# The 9.9%
# FAT-FREE
# Cookbook

Doubleday

NEW YORK   LONDON
TORONTO
SYDNEY   AUCKLAND

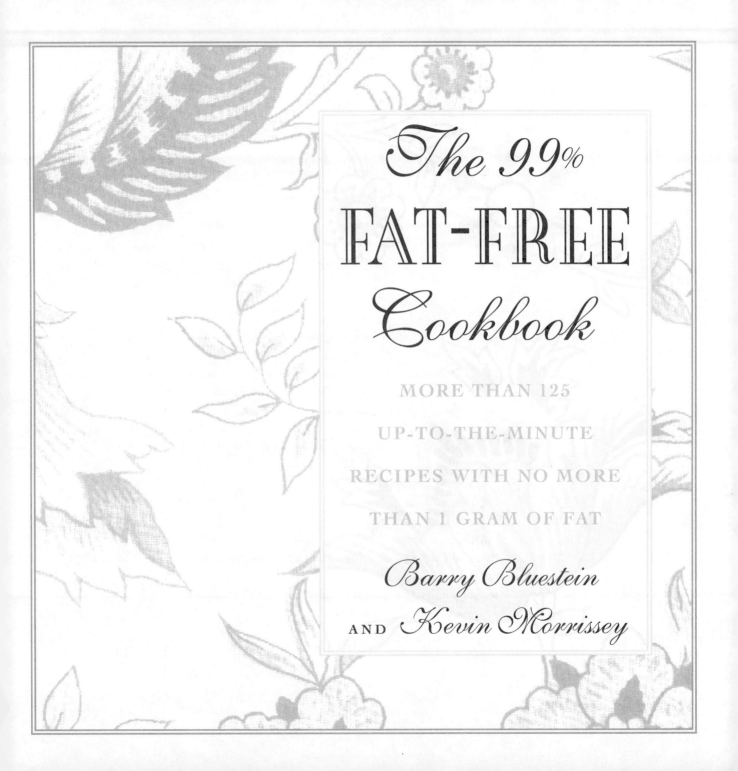

# The 99% FAT-FREE Cookbook

MORE THAN 125

UP-TO-THE-MINUTE

RECIPES WITH NO MORE

THAN 1 GRAM OF FAT

*Barry Bluestein*

AND *Kevin Morrissey*

PUBLISHED BY DOUBLEDAY

a division of Bantam Doubleday Dell Publishing Group, Inc.

1540 Broadway, New York, New York 10036

DOUBLEDAY and the portrayal of an anchor with a dolphin
are trademarks of Doubleday,
a division of Bantam Doubleday Dell Publishing Group, Inc.

Book design by Marysarah Quinn

Library of Congress Cataloging-in-Publication Data
Bluestein, Barry.
    The 99% fat-free cookbook : more than 125 up-to-the-minute recipes
with no more than 1 gram of fat / Barry Bluestein and Kevin
Morrissey. — 1st ed.
        p.      cm.
    1. Low-fat diet—Recipes.    I. Morrissey, Kevin.    II. Title.
III.  Title: Ninety-nine percent fat free cookbook.
    RM237.7.B58   1994
    641.5′638—dc20                                        93-25293
                                                              CIP

ISBN 0-385-47019-3
Copyright © 1994 by Barry Bluestein and Kevin Morrissey
All Rights Reserved
Printed in the United States of America
April 1994


10   9   8   7   6

DEDICATED TO

*Jeff Wilson*

WHO WAS ALWAYS THERE

# Acknowl-edgments

We gratefully acknowledge the assistance of Lisa Schumacher Newkirk, Claudia Clark Potter, Colin Reeves, William Rice, and Jill Van Cleave for their ideas and advice as this book took shape. For their help in recipe development and testing, we would like to thank Ann Bloomstrand and Elaine Brooks, our bread maven in the Berkshires.

Elaine Barlas earned a special place in paradise for her dual role of culinary cheerleader and sous chef for our tastings. Appreciation for their constructive feedback goes to our panel of tasters, who included: Ricardo Alcaraz, Bob and Jo Ann Bassi, Harry and Eleanor Bluestein, Cheryl Blumenthal, Linda Gray, Jerry and Pat Grose, Rob Humrickhouse, John Koulias, Marlis Levin, Emmie and Bill Ruffin, Art Smith, Greg Snider, and John Vranicar.

We extend heartfelt thanks to Judith Kern, our editor, without whose vision and knowledge our idea would not be a book. Lastly, we acknowledge the contributions of Carol Siegel, for her thoughtful copy editing, and of Susan Ramer, our always supportive literary agent.

# Contents

# Introduction

The American way of eating has changed irrevocably during the past decade. The pursuit of a lighter and more healthful diet has become the driving force behind a quiet but steady revolution taking place in homes across the nation.

The new passion for setting a healthful dining table has entered the mainstream with a vengeance. As a people, we are finally taking heed of a generation of scientific data demonstrating the links between the traditional, high-fat American diet and numerous preventable, dietary-related health problems.

Long conscious of the need to limit our intake of so-called fattening foods, we are now learning the very important distinction between simple calories and the fat content of the foods we eat. We are quickly coming to appreciate that counting calories without looking at fat content is to focus on the battle while disregarding the war.

Yet there is a troubling lag between acquiring knowledge and learning to use it. Even as "fat free" has become the rallying slogan for the marketing of commercially prepared synthetic products, home cooks struggling to eliminate fat in the preparation of fresh, natural foods labor methodically to revise individual recipes. The majority of cookbooks now on the market provide little in the way of an overall guiding technique; and the majority of recipes, even in those books with a "light" or "healthy-eating" focus, still contain at least 5 or 10 grams of fat per serving.

We believe the problem is a basic conceptual one: Simply stated, we must learn to cook fat free in order to eat fat free. Most recipes rely on traditional cooking methods, which require the use of fatty ingredients. Revisions that purport to be light in most cases simply reduce the amount of fat used in the recipe or downscale the size of the portion—the culinary equivalent of the old binge-and-starve approach to dieting.

Just as we have learned to pursue a more healthful diet by changing our everyday eating habits, we must learn to prepare more healthful food by changing our cooking techniques. The next logical step in the dietary revolution is to shift responsibility for fat-free eating from the dining table to the kitchen.

## The 99% Fat-Free Kitchen

In the *The 99% Fat-Free Cookbook*, we offer a guiding philosophy and simple techniques for eliminating as much fat as possible at the source, your kitchen. We include only recipes with 1 gram of fat or less per serving.

Our premise that fat-free eating derives from fat-free cooking requires reeducating the cook, not depriving the diner. In testing recipes for this book, we found that most of our guests did not realize the dishes we served them were fat free until we told them so.

Fat-free cooking entails discriminating selection and innovative preparation of ingredients, not deletion of favorite dishes from our menus. Essentially, we have broken traditional recipes and methodologies down to their basic components and rebuilt them in ways that eliminate superfluous fats—fats that contribute little to—and may even mask—intrinsic flavor.

It's not necessary to banish chocolate recipes from the fat-free kitchen, just to avoid the use of cocoa butter in their preparation. Cakes and cookies can be made without butter, cream, and egg yolks. You don't have to sacrifice roux-based dishes, as long the roux is made without fat. While the fat content of red meat is too high for inclusion in fat-free recipes, poultry and seafood can be used judiciously to enhance flavor and texture.

Think of the common use of fats in everyday cooking as a troublesome habit to be broken. Why, for example, must we automatically reach for that fat-laden bottle of oil every time we perform as basic a first step as sautéing? The oil isn't necessary and may well make the difference between keeping the subsequent recipe in a healthy-cooking repertoire or discarding it. Substituting canola oil for vegetable oil is no answer; it merely begs the more fundamental question.

While no one can—or should—eliminate *all* fat, few now disagree that a major overhaul of the fatty American diet is essential. *The 99% Fat-Free Cookbook* offers a painless approach for trimming gratuitous fat from meals. Use it as a guide and as a point of departure. If you systematically work 99% fat-free recipes into your cooking repertoire, you will reduce substantially the fat content of the table you set in no time—allowing for a rich and varied menu and enabling the occasional splurge without undue guilt.

# 99% Fat-Free Cooking Techniques

Replacing traditional cooking methods with fat-free techniques is fundamental. Detailed recipe directions build on a few basic concepts, which include:

- **BAKING:** Oil, shortening, and egg yolks are not needed. We substitute egg whites, fruit purees, buttermilk, and light corn syrup.

- **BINDING:** We use potato or vegetable purees or egg whites rather than whole eggs to bind savory cakes and fillings.

- **BROWNING:** We use juice, stock, or bread crumbs in place of melted butter and oil.

- **FLAVORING:** To achieve the smoky taste usually derived from the inclusion of ham or pork, we cook with a little smoked turkey or steam ingredients with a few bacon cubes added to the water in the bottom of the steamer. In desserts, sauces, and dressings, we use buttermilk for the rich, creamy taste of butter.

- **FRYING:** Slow baking, which imparts the same crispness as frying to many foods, is our preferred method. It is done dry or with a touch of light cooking spray, eliminating the heavy oils needed for frying.

- **GLISTENING:** The gloss on a bowl of pasta usually comes from tossing the noodles in oil, and the sheen of a sauce usually comes from one of a variety of fats. We toss pastas in stock, instead, and finish sauces with a little stock and corn-starch.

⊲  **SAUTÉING:** Instead of using oil, butter, or shortening over medium to high heat, we "sweat" vegetables over low heat, which releases their own moisture, or add just a little water. For seafood and poultry, we use water, stock, or other fat-free liquid, also over low heat.

⊲  **THICKENING:** To thicken soups, sauces, and stews, we re-place butter and flour with either vegetable purees or but-termilk. For salad dressings that cling, we use corn syrup or honey instead of oil.

1

# The 99%
# FAT-FREE
# Pantry

## A Word on Counts, Portions, and Equivalents

Total fat per serving has been calculated for each recipe to the nearest $\frac{1}{100}$th of a gram. For commercial products, we use the lowest-fat brands readily available. Counts are based to the greatest extent possible on actual data rather than on the liberally rounded off figures manufacturers have sometimes used on product labels. Recently standardized federal labeling guidelines should help consumers in their selection of commercial products. Read and compare product labels carefully.

Although serving sizes vary some among the recipes, we have tried to maintain consistent portions, averaging 6 to 8 ounces for main courses.

To give you a better idea how much to buy at the market, equivalents are provided for ingredient measures, unless the measured item is too small, that is, less than a whole. For example:

1 cup chopped white onion (1 medium onion);
½ tablespoon chopped garlic (about 2 cloves);
2 large red bell peppers (14 to 16 ounces total);
4 cups cubed red potatoes (about 1½ pounds potatoes).

## The Pantry

**BACON SMOKING:** In several recipes, we impart the smoky flavor of pork products, without the fat, by cooking ingredients in a steamer and adding cubed bacon to the water in the bottom of the steamer. The trick is to make sure the water level is low enough so as not to bubble up through the holes in the bottom of the steamer basket, since you don't want the fat from the bacon to come into contact with the ingredients above. Use real smoked, not cured, bacon for its strong flavor.

Smoked turkey skin works as well as smoked bacon for this purpose and can be frozen for convenient storage.

**BASIL VINEGAR:** To make basil vinegar, add 4 to 6 sprigs fresh basil for every 3 cups white wine vinegar and set aside in a clean jar for about 1 week.

**BEANS:** A few of our recipes call for canned beans because there are commercial products available that have less fat than beans cooked at home. This is the case with butter beans, garbanzo beans, and kidney beans. Compare product labels.

**BREAD CRUMBS:** As all of the prepared bread crumbs we've found have a higher fat content than we budgeted for this ingredient, we make our own. One slice of white, Italian, or oatmeal sandwich bread yields 4 to 5 tablespoons bread crumbs. Break up the bread into the bowl of a food processor and pulse a few times to make uniform-sized crumbs. Compare the fat content of "light" breads now available from commercial manufacturers.

**CHICKEN STOCK:** We strongly recommend that you use 99% Fat Free Chicken Stock (page 10), because making your own provides greater control over taste and fat content. If you do use commercial chicken stock, refrigerate it and then skim and strain before heating, according to our recipe directions.

**COCOA POWDER:** Our recipes are based upon the use of Dutch-processed cocoa powder, which produces a different chemical reaction from other cocoas, which are not treated with an alkali. Compare product labels among Dutch or European-style cocoa powders, which vary in fat content.

**CORN:** As canned or frozen corn contains less fat than fresh, we call for these varieties in recipes where their use makes a significant difference in fat content without appreciably affecting taste. Compare product labels.

**EGG SUBSTITUTE AND EGG WHITE:** We use liquid egg substitute a lot for convenience and shelf life (it can be stored in the freezer and kept far longer than shell eggs). Brands that are "nonfat" are clearly marked as such; these are pasteurized egg products from which the fatty yolks have been removed. For those recipes in which we specifically call for egg white, egg substitute should not be used. An equal volume of egg white may be used if you prefer in all recipes calling for liquid egg substitute, with the exception of the Pasta Frittata (page 90), which needs the color provided by the egg substitute.

**GROUND TURKEY:** Don't use packaged preground turkey, which contains a considerable amount of fat. Have your butcher grind trimmed turkey breast, or prepare it yourself using a meat grinder or the grinder attachment to a stationary electric mixer or food processor.

**PASTA:** We make our own pasta (page 7), which is very low in fat; if you buy commercially prepared pasta, buy a "light" variety and compare product labels.

**PEAS:** Some recipes call for canned or frozen peas because these have less fat than fresh peas.

**SALT:** We often call for coarse kosher salt, which can be used in all but baking recipes. Readily available in most supermarkets, kosher salt has less sodium per measure than finer-grain table salt.

**SUN-DRIED TOMATOES:** Sun-dried tomatoes can be purchased already prepared, or you can make them at home. To dry your own tomatoes, preheat the oven to 140 degrees. Cut plum tomatoes in half lengthwise and place them on a cookie sheet, cut side up. Bake for about 18 hours, until the tomatoes are dry, deep reddish brown in color, and still somewhat elastic. Do not allow them to blacken or become brittle.

**TOMATOES:** Since fresh tomatoes do contain more fat, we call for canned tomatoes (preferably the Italian pear or plum variety) when necessary to keep the fat content of a particular recipe at an acceptable level. Canned tomatoes are actually preferable to hothouse tomatoes, since they are allowed to ripen longer on the vine.

**TORTILLAS:** The fat content of corn tortillas varies widely. Read nutritional labels carefully.

**WHITE RICE:** Several brands of long-grain white rice are well within our guidelines for fat content if cooked without butter.

**YOGURT CHEESE:** To make yogurt cheese, suspend a yogurt funnel (available from kitchenware stores) or a strainer that has been lined with a coffee filter atop a nonreactive bowl. Empty plain nonfat yogurt into the funnel or strainer and place the bowl in the refrigerator for at least 8 hours, preferably overnight, until all the liquid whey has dripped through into the bowl. The substance remaining in the funnel or strainer is pure yogurt cheese.

# Homemade Pasta

2 cups all-purpose flour, plus a little extra for flouring during preparation

¼ cup nonfat liquid egg substitute

Put the flour into the bowl of a food processor. Pulse while adding the egg substitute. This will produce a soft ball of dough.

Turn out onto a floured board and knead the dough into a single ball that is glossy and elastic. Enclose in plastic wrap and set aside for 30 minutes.

Flour the rollers of a pasta machine. Cut the dough in quarters, flour all over, and flatten. Put the first piece of dough through the largest opening on the pasta machine 3 times, folding the dough in half after each time through. Then put it through each successively smaller opening, until it has gone through the smallest. Repeat this process for the remaining 3 pieces of dough.

Put each of the thin pieces of dough through the wide cutters on the pasta machine. Hang and dry the strands of pasta for about 10 minutes.

*Yield—1 pound*

# 99% Fat-Free Smoked Turkey Stock

3 pounds smoked turkey bones, with a few
   scraps of meat left on
1 large yellow onion, peels reserved
1 tomato, quartered; or 3 plum tomatoes,
   halved

2 unpeeled carrots, trimmed and halved
   lengthwise
2 stalks celery, trimmed and halved
4 bay leaves
About 5 quarts water

Preheat the oven to 450 degrees.

Place the turkey bones in an aluminum foil–lined baking pan just large enough to hold them all in a single layer. Bake for about 30 minutes, until the bones are very brown, turning once after 15 minutes. Remove from the baking pan and place on paper towels to drain off any remaining fat.

Meanwhile, put the vegetables into a second baking pan and bake for 20 minutes, turning once after 10 minutes.

Put the baked turkey bones, vegetables, reserved onion peels, and the bay leaves into a large stockpot. Cover with the water. Bring to a rapid boil over high heat and skim the foamy residue off the top. Turn the heat down to low and simmer, uncovered, for about 4 hours, periodically skimming the residue off the top.

Remove from the heat and discard all the solid ingredients. Be sure to remove the bay leaves. Strain the liquid into a large bowl and refrigerate, uncovered, for at least 2 to 3 hours. If refrigerating overnight, cover after 2 to 3 hours.

Remove the stock from the refrigerator and, using a large spoon, lift off the layer of fat that has settled on top. Then, scrape along the top of the stock with a dinner knife to catch any small pieces of fat still remaining. Return the stock to a large pot and cook over medium heat for 2 to 3 minutes, until the stock has liquefied. Pour the liquefied stock through a strainer lined with a double layer of cheesecloth into a clean bowl.

The turkey stock will keep for 3 days in the refrigerator or 6 months in the freezer. We freeze it in 2– and 4–cup portions in resealable plastic bags.

*Yield—about 1⅔ quarts*

# 99% Fat-Free
# Chicken Stock

4 pounds chicken bones, with a few scraps
   of meat left on
3 unpeeled carrots, trimmed and cut
   into chunks
2 unpeeled parsnips, trimmed and
   quartered lengthwise

1 large yellow onion, cut into 1-inch
   chunks
5 stalks celery, trimmed and quartered
15 sprigs fresh parsley, ends trimmed
About 5 quarts water
12 whole black peppercorns

Put the chicken bones, vegetables, and parsley in a large stockpot. Cover with the water. Bring to a rapid boil over high heat, then skim the foamy residue off the top. Reduce the heat to low and simmer for about 4 hours, uncovered, until the bones begin to disintegrate. Periodically skim the residue off the top.

Remove the pot from the heat. Discard all the solid ingredients and strain the liquid into a large bowl. Add the peppercorns and refrigerate, uncovered, for at least 2 to 3 hours. If refrigerating overnight, cover after 2 to 3 hours.

When you take the stock out of the refrigerator, use a large spoon to lift off the layer of fat that has settled on top. Then, using a dinner knife, scrape along the top of the stock to catch any small pieces of fat still remaining. Place the stock in a large pot and cook over medium heat for 2 to 3 minutes, until the stock has liquefied. Pour the liquefied stock through a strainer lined with a double layer of cheesecloth (to strain the sediment) into a clean bowl.

The chicken stock will keep for 3 days in the refrigerator or 6 months in the freezer. We freeze it in 2– and 4–cup portions in resealable plastic bags.

*Yield — about 1⅔ quarts*

2

*First*

# COURSES

# Corn Crabcakes with Cayenne Cream

CRABCAKES:

8 ounces uncooked crabmeat
1 large egg, white only
About 5 tablespoons homemade bread
   crumbs (see Pantry)
⅓ cup corn kernels
3 drops hot sauce
½ tablespoon freshly squeezed lemon juice
1 teaspoon Dijon mustard
⅛ teaspoon freshly ground black pepper
1 tablespoon nonfat sour cream
1 teaspoon Worcestershire sauce

CAYENNE CREAM:

¼ cup plain nonfat yogurt
¼ cup nonfat sour cream
1½ tablespoons minced cornichons
1 tablespoon minced fresh parsley
⅛ teaspoon cayenne pepper
⅛ teaspoon freshly ground black pepper
2 teaspoons freshly squeezed lemon juice

Rinse the crabmeat in a colander under cold running water, picking out any filament or shell. Squeeze out any excess water.

Combine all the crabcake ingredients in a large bowl and mix well. Scoop out a generous 2 tablespoons, roll as you would a meatball, and flatten into a cake. Repeat until you have formed 8 cakes. Place the crabcakes on a nonstick baking sheet, cover, and refrigerate for 30 minutes.

Preheat the oven to 450 degrees.

Bake the crabcakes for about 20 minutes, until golden, flip, and bake for about 10 minutes on the other side.

Meanwhile, combine all the ingredients for the cayenne cream and mix until thoroughly blended.

For each portion, serve 2 crabcakes with a little cayenne cream on the side.

Yield—4 servings
Fat per serving—0.95 g.

# Tricolor Peppers on Garlic-Polenta Crostini

This dish is unique in both appearance and texture—a bright multicolored splash of chilled pepper served atop a pinwheel of warm, pale crostini made from polenta rather than bread.

**PEPPERS:**

2 large red bell peppers (about 14 ounces total), halved lengthwise and seeded

2 large green bell peppers, halved lengthwise and seeded

2 large yellow bell peppers, halved lengthwise and seeded

4 cloves garlic

¼ cup balsamic vinegar

½ cup chopped fresh basil

1 teaspoon sugar

1 teaspoon salt

1 teaspoon freshly ground black pepper

**CROSTINI:**

3 cloves garlic, quartered

¼ cup water

2 cups skim milk

⅔ cup buttermilk

¼ teaspoon salt

1 teaspoon sugar

1 cup instant polenta

Preheat the broiler and cover the rack with aluminum foil.

Place the bell peppers on the rack, cut side down, 2 to 3 inches from the heat source. Broil for about 5 minutes, until charred. Remove carefully and seal in an airtight plastic bag. Let cool for about 10 minutes.

Remove the peppers from the plastic bag, rub off the skin, slice into narrow strips, and set aside in a nonreactive bowl.

With a press, crush the garlic cloves into a small bowl. Add the remaining ingredients. Mix until the sugar is completely dissolved. Pour this mixture over the sliced peppers and mix well, making sure the peppers are thoroughly coated. Cover and chill in the refrigerator for 2 hours, to allow the flavors to meld.

To make the crostini, put the quartered garlic and water in a small saucepan and bring to a boil over medium heat. Cover, lower the heat, and simmer for about 10 minutes, until the garlic is tender.

Transfer the contents of the saucepan to a small bowl and mash the garlic with a fork. The mixture will not be completely smooth but should be free of any large pieces of garlic.

Combine the skim milk, buttermilk, salt, and sugar in a saucepan and bring to a simmer over medium heat. Whisk in the mashed garlic. Slowly add the instant polenta while whisking, then lower the heat. Continue to cook for about 5 minutes, stirring with a wooden spoon, until the mixture is thick, smooth, and separates easily from the sides of the pan.

Pour into a nonstick 8-inch loaf pan, cover, and refrigerate for 2 hours.

Preheat the grill or broiler.

Remove the polenta from the pan and cut it into ½-inch slices. Cut each slice in half on the diagonal. Grill or broil 1 to 2 minutes per side, until brown. If using the grill, you may want to brown the short sides as well, 30 seconds to 1 minute each.

For each portion, serve 4 pieces of grilled polenta placed on the plate in a pinwheel arrangement and topped with chilled marinated pepper slices.

*Yield — 8 servings*
*Fat per serving — 0.92 g.*

## Shrimp with Chayote and Snow Peas

1 cup peeled, chopped chayote
4 ounces snow peas, trimmed and cut into
   thirds on the diagonal
3 ½ ounces cooked shrimp, peeled, deveined,
   and halved
½ red onion, sliced into half rounds
   (about ¾ cup)

1 tablespoon stone-ground mustard
1 tablespoon champagne vinegar
2 tablespoons plain nonfat yogurt
½ tablespoon sugar

Bring a saucepan half filled with water to a boil. Add the chayote and boil for 10 minutes. Add the pea pods and cook for another 20 seconds. Drain and rinse the vegetables immediately under cold running water. Transfer to a bowl and add the shrimp and onion.

In a small bowl, combine the mustard and vinegar. Whisk in the yogurt, then the sugar.

Pour the dressing over the shrimp mixture and toss to coat all ingredients well. Chill for at least 1 hour before serving.

*Yield—4 servings*
*Fat per serving—0.70 g.*

# Mushroom Strudel

8 ounces white button mushrooms
8 ounces portobello mushrooms
¼ teaspoon chopped fresh tarragon
⅛ teaspoon freshly grated nutmeg
⅛ teaspoon freshly ground black pepper

½ teaspoon salt
1 cup evaporated skim milk
4 sheets phyllo dough (about 3 ounces)
¼ cup 99% Fat-Free Chicken Stock
   (page 10)

Clean and slice the mushrooms. Put them in a nonstick frying pan and cook for 4 minutes over medium heat, stirring constantly. Stir in the tarragon, nutmeg, pepper, and salt. Add the evaporated milk. Lower the heat and simmer for about 15 minutes, uncovered, until the liquid thickens.

Transfer to a food processor or blender and puree. Cover and refrigerate for 30 minutes to thicken and chill.

Preheat the oven to 375 degrees.

Lay out the sheets of phyllo dough and cover with a slightly dampened towel during assembly.

Cut a piece of baker's parchment to fit a baking sheet, then lay it on the countertop. Lay a rectangular sheet of phyllo dough lengthwise on the paper and paint it with chicken stock.

Lay a second sheet, and then a third, directly on top, painting each with stock after positioning. Lay the remaining sheet on top, but do not paint it.

Spoon the mushroom filling onto a short end of the phyllo rectangle, covering about a quarter of the dough and leaving a ¼-inch outer border. Lift the outer edge alongside the filling and roll the dough over onto itself to form a log. Carefully reposition the log so that it rests lengthwise on the baker's parchment, seam side down. Transfer the paper and log to the baking sheet. Paint the exposed dough surface with the remaining chicken stock.

Bake for about 30 minutes, until golden.

Slice into 6 portions.

*Yield—6 servings*
*Fat per serving—0.56 g.*

This versatile savory pastry also works well as a side dish to accompany poultry. Don't be intimidated by the idea of working with phyllo dough; it's really quite easy. The amount of white mushrooms called for can be doubled if portobello aren't available.

# Fish Sausage
## with Fennel Sauce

The use of plastic wrap in this recipe to form the sausages and hold them together during cooking replaces the laborious preparation steps in traditional recipes. We're partial to fennel sauce atop this sausage, but try Roasted Red Pepper Cream (page 30) instead if you don't have a juice extractor, necessary for preparing the fennel sauce.

FISH SAUSAGE:
One 8-ounce uncooked cod fillet, quartered
2 tablespoons homemade bread crumbs
    (see Pantry)
Pinch of cayenne pepper
2 tablespoons chopped fresh parsley
1 tablespoon brandy
¼ cup nonfat liquid egg substitute,
    lightly beaten
½ cup evaporated skim milk
4 ounces uncooked scallops

¼ cup trimmed, finely chopped scallions
    (2–3 scallions)
4 sheets heavy plastic wrap, for poaching
    sausage

FENNEL SAUCE:
2 large fennel bulbs (about
    1¾ pounds total)
2 teaspoons cornstarch
½ teaspoon freshly squeezed lemon juice

To make the sausage, put the cod, bread crumbs, cayenne pepper, parsley, and brandy into the bowl of a food processor. Turn on the machine and immediately add the egg substitute, then the evaporated milk, through the feed tube. Turn off the machine and add the scallops. Process for 15 seconds.

Transfer the mixture to a bowl and fold in the scallions. Cover and chill in the refrigerator for 1 hour.

Spread a sheet of heavy plastic wrap on the countertop. Put a quarter of the chilled fish mixture at one end of the sheet and roll it into a sausage-shaped log about 3 inches long and 1 inch thick. Twist the ends of the plastic wrap closed. Repeat with the remaining plastic and fish.

Fill a deep-sided sauté pan at least halfway with water and bring to a boil over medium heat. Lower the heat, put the plastic-encased sausages into the water, and bring back to a bare simmer. Cover and poach for 10 minutes.

Remove the sausages with a slotted spoon and allow them to cool for 10 minutes. Unwrap and slice each sausage into 4 rounds about ¾ inch long.

For the sauce, trim the fennel bulbs, reserving the leaves. Cut each bulb into 5 slices lengthwise, then cut each slice in half. Put the pieces through a juice extractor. (This should produce about 2 cups fennel juice.)

Snip enough of the fennel leaves to yield 2 tablespoons and set aside.

Put the cornstarch into a bowl and mix in 4 teaspoons of the fennel juice.

Combine the lemon juice and the remaining fennel juice in a saucepan and cook for about 3 minutes over medium heat, until just beginning to boil. Remove from the heat, whisk, then add the dissolved cornstarch while still whisking. Return to low heat and cook for about 2 minutes, whisking constantly, until the mixture begins to thicken. Stir in the 2 tablespoons of fennel leaves. Continue to cook for about 3 minutes, stirring with a spoon, until fully thickened to sauce consistency.

Serve 4 rounds of fish sausage on each plate, with some of the fennel sauce drizzled on top.

*Yield—4 servings*
*Fat per serving—0.95 g.*

# Squid with Pasta

Most fish markets sell cleaned squid, which makes preparation almost effortless. Be sure not to overcook the squid, as this will toughen the naturally tender meat.

12 ounces cleaned, trimmed squid (bodies and tentacles)

1 cup chopped white onion (about 1 medium onion)

One 28-ounce can peeled Italian-style plum tomatoes, seeded and chopped, juice reserved

½ tablespoon minced garlic (about 2 cloves)

1 cup seeded, chopped yellow bell pepper (about 1 medium bell pepper)

½ cup dry red wine

2 teaspoons chopped fresh oregano

1 tablespoon tomato paste

5 ounces uncooked thin-strand pasta (see Pantry)

Slice the squid bodies into ¼-inch rings.

In a saucepan, combine the onion and 4 tablespoons of the juice from the tomatoes and sauté for about 6 minutes over medium-low heat, until the onion is wilted. Add the garlic and bell pepper and cook for another 2 minutes.

Add the wine, squid, chopped tomatoes, the remaining juice from the tomatoes, the oregano, and the tomato paste. Raise the heat to high and bring to a boil. Cover and boil for 5 minutes, then reduce the heat to low and simmer for 45 minutes.

Remove the cover and continue to simmer for about 15 minutes longer, until the sauce thickens.

While the squid simmers, bring a large pot of water to a boil, add the pasta, and cook to desired tenderness (3 to 4 minutes for homemade or other fresh pasta, 8 to 10 minutes for dry). Drain the pasta, distribute it among 6 pasta bowls, and top each portion with equal amounts (about 7 ounces each) of the squid mixture.

*Yield — 6 servings*
*Fat per serving — 0.99 g.*

# Hummus with Sweet Potato Chips

**HUMMUS:**

8 ounces canned garbanzo beans, drained
    and rinsed
½ cup plain nonfat yogurt
3 tablespoons freshly squeezed lemon juice
3 tablespoons chopped flat-leaf parsley
⅛ teaspoon ground cumin
2 cloves garlic

**SWEET POTATO CHIPS:**

1 pound sweet potato, peeled
Light vegetable oil cooking spray
1 tablespoon seasoned salt

This is an extremely light and refreshing hummus, made without fat-laden tahini and oil. We call for the use of a blender to puree the hummus because it yields a smoother consistency; if chunkier hummus is desired, use a food processor. Sweet potato chips can burn quickly and require more diligent watching than is needed for oven roasting white potatoes, but they are well worth the extra effort.

Preheat the oven to 300 degrees.

For the hummus, combine the beans, yogurt, lemon juice, parsley, and cumin in the bowl of a blender. Press in the garlic and puree until smooth. (This should yield about 1 cup of hummus.)

Thinly slice the sweet potato, using a mandoline slicer.

Lightly spray a nonstick baking sheet twice with the vegetable oil spray and rub the oil evenly over the surface. Arrange the potato slices on the baking sheet in a single layer and place in the oven.

After 5 minutes, sprinkle about half the seasoned salt over the potatoes. After another 5 minutes, turn the slices and salt the other side. When the potatoes have cooked a total of 15 minutes, remove any browned chips. Flip the uncooked slices and move them to the outer edges of the pan. It may take another 5 minutes to cook all the chips. (This should yield about 90 chips.)

Serve the hummus in a bowl centered on a large plate, surrounded by sweet potato chips.

*Yield — 6 servings*
*Fat per serving — 0.85 g.*

# Lobster Tostadas

The sublime decadence of lobster paired with the earthy tortilla makes a wonderful Sunday brunch item. Serve these with jalapeño-spiked Bloody Marys.

SALSA:

1 small jalapeño pepper, halved and seeded
1 small white onion (about 3 ounces), halved
1 large clove garlic
½ cup fresh cilantro leaves
3 red plum tomatoes (about 6 ounces total), cored and quartered
1 yellow tomato (about 6 ounces), cored and quartered
2 teaspoons freshly squeezed lime juice

Four 6-inch corn tortillas
6 tablespoons dry white wine
12 ounces cooked lobster meat, sliced
6 large leaves red-leaf lettuce, shredded

Preheat the oven to 375 degrees.

For the salsa, put the jalapeño pepper, onion, garlic, and ¼ cup of the cilantro into the bowl of a food processor and process to a fine mince. Add the red and yellow tomatoes and pulse to a coarse chop. Transfer to a bowl, stir in the lime juice, and set aside.

Put the tortillas into the oven directly on the middle rack. Bake for about 5 minutes, until toasted.

Meanwhile, combine the remaining ¼ cup cilantro and the wine in a nonstick frying pan. Cook for 1 minute over low heat, just until the liquid begins to smoke. Stir in the lobster meat, cover, and cook for 3 minutes. Remove from the heat.

Put the toasted tortillas on individual serving plates, topped with a handful of lettuce. Divide the salsa and lobster meat among the 4 tostadas, and spoon a little of the cilantro and wine mixture over each serving.

Yield—4 servings
Fat per serving—0.91 g.

# Zucchini Ravioli with Caramelized Onion and Roasted Tomato Sauce

DOUGH:

2 cups all-purpose flour, plus a little extra
    for flouring during preparation
1 cup nonfat liquid egg substitute

FILLING:

¼ cup finely chopped yellow onion
¼ cup water
1 teaspoon minced garlic (about 1
    large clove)
2 cups peeled, diced zucchini (about 1
    large zucchini)
¼ teaspoon dried oregano
Pinch of freshly ground black pepper
¼ teaspoon salt
½ cup homemade bread crumbs
    (see Pantry)
1 tablespoon nonfat liquid egg substitute

SAUCE:

2 large tomatoes (about 1 pound total)
2 cups thinly sliced white onion
    (about 1 large or 2 small)
½ cup plus 3 tablespoons freshly squeezed
    orange juice
1½ cups water
⅛ teaspoon dried thyme

ASSEMBLY:

2 tablespoons nonfat liquid egg substitute
1 teaspoon water

We assemble and freeze the ravioli to cook on cold winter nights that beg for hearty, satisfying, one-course meals. As a dinner for two, the portions contain more than 1 gram fat, but are nonetheless light and healthful. Put the fresh ravioli into the freezer in a single layer on a cookie sheet and transfer to a large airtight bag once they are frozen.

To make the dough, put the flour into the bowl of a food processor. Turn the machine on and slowly pour the egg substitute through the feed tube. Process until all the liquid has been absorbed, forming a ball of dough.

Remove the dough and knead for 1 minute. Enclose in plastic wrap and set aside.

For the filling, combine the chopped onion and the water in a nonstick frying pan. Cook for 8 minutes over the lowest possible heat. Add the garlic and cook for about 2 minutes, stirring con-

stantly, until almost all the water is absorbed. Add the zucchini and cook, stirring, for 1 minute more. Stir in the oregano, pepper, and salt. Cover and cook for about 20 minutes, until the zucchini is very soft.

Remove from the heat, scrape the mixture into the bowl of a food processor or blender, and puree to a very soft consistency.

Transfer to a mixing bowl. Mix in the bread crumbs and egg substitute, blending well. Cover and refrigerate until ready to use.

Preheat the oven to 400 degrees.

To make the sauce, place the tomatoes in a shallow baking dish lined with aluminum foil. Put them in the oven and roast for 50 minutes.

Meanwhile, preheat a nonstick frying pan over medium heat. Add the sliced onion and cook for about 8 minutes, stirring constantly, until the onion becomes dry and begins to stick to the pan. Stir in 1 tablespoon of the orange juice and cook for 5 minutes. Add another tablespoon of orange juice, stir, and cook for an additional 5 minutes. Stir in a third tablespoon of orange juice and cook for about 2 minutes more, stirring constantly, until the liquid is totally absorbed and the onion is golden. Remove from the heat and transfer to a food processor or blender.

When the tomatoes are done and cool enough to handle, cut out the cores and add the tomatoes to the onion in the food processor or blender. Puree until smooth.

Return the puree to the frying pan. Cook for 10 to 12 minutes over medium heat, stirring occasionally, until the mixture is thick and dry. Remove from the heat and stir in the water, the remaining ½ cup orange juice, and the thyme.

Return to the heat and bring to a boil. Lower the heat and simmer for 20 minutes, until the mixture is reduced by about a third to a saucelike consistency. Remove from the heat.

To make the ravioli, flour the rollers of a pasta machine. Unwrap the dough, cut it in thirds, and then cut each third in half. Flour and flatten each piece of dough.

Put one piece of dough through the largest opening on the pasta machine 3 times, folding it in half after each time through.

Then put it through each successively smaller opening, until it has gone through the smallest. Repeat for each of the remaining pieces of dough.

Place 3 of the flat, rectangular sheets of dough on a countertop. Onto each sheet, scoop 12 small mounds of filling (½ teaspoonful for each mound) spaced 1½ inches apart. Whisk the egg substitute with the water and paint all of the exposed dough surface with this mixture.

Top each with a second sheet of dough. Pressing down firmly with the side of your hand, make indentations in the dough, equally spaced between the mounds, to form the borders of the 12 ravioli on each sheet. Cut along the indentations to separate the ravioli. (The prepared ravioli can be frozen at this point. See head note.)

Bring a large pot of water to a boil. Drop in the ravioli and cook over medium heat for about 5 minutes. When the ravioli rise to the surface of the boiling water, they are done.

While the ravioli are cooking, reheat the sauce over low heat.

Serve 6 ravioli per person and spoon some of the sauce over each serving.

*Yield — 6 servings*
*Fat per serving — 0.80 g.*

# Stuffed Squid Rings

3 sun-dried tomatoes (see Pantry)
1 clove garlic
3 cups boiling water
3 large spinach leaves, washed and stemmed
3 large cleaned squid with tentacles (about 3 ounces)

½ cup cooked white rice
1 teaspoon chopped scallion
½ cup white wine
¼ cup soy sauce

Combine the tomatoes, garlic, and ⅓ cup of the boiling water and set aside to steep.

Put the spinach leaves in a colander, pour the rest of the boiling water over them, and let drain.

Remove the reconstituted tomatoes from the soaking liquid and sliver them.

To make the stuffing, cut up the squid tentacles and mix them with the rice, scallion, and slivered tomatoes. Divide this mixture among the 3 spinach leaves. Roll each spinach leaf and stuff it into a squid. Secure closed with toothpicks.

Bring the wine and soy sauce to a boil in a saucepan. Add the stuffed squid to the saucepan, lower the heat, cover, and simmer for about 25 minutes, until they are fork tender.

Refrigerate the stuffed squid for 15 minutes, then cut each one into 4 rings. Serve 3 rings per person.

*Yield — 4 servings*
*Fat per serving — 0.42 g.*

# Tequila Scallops

8 ounces uncooked bay scallops
¼ cup tequila
2 tablespoons freshly squeezed lime juice
1 medium ruby red grapefruit, peeled and
   cut into segments, juice reserved
   (collected juice from seeding and
   sectioning grapefruit should yield
   about ¼ cup)

4 teaspoons chopped fresh cilantro,
   for garnish

*Now you can have your ceviche and heat it too, a good thing given the emerging health concerns about eating raw seafood.*

Combine the scallops, tequila, and lime juice in a nonstick frying pan. Sauté for about 5 minutes over medium heat, until the scallops are firm and opaque. Transfer to a plate with a slotted spoon.

Add the grapefruit juice to the pan, lower the heat, and simmer for 2 to 3 minutes, until the liquid is reduced by about half and thickened.

Add the grapefruit segments and scallops. Toss to mix, remove from the heat, and serve garnished with cilantro.

*Yield—4 servings*
*Fat per serving—0.46 g.*

# Cold Vegetable Terrine in Basil Aspic

We like to slice and plate the terrine so that the exposed layers of vibrantly colored vegetables lend a warm welcoming feel to the dinner table. The terrine can also be served whole for a dramatic buffet presentation. The addition of basil to the aspic water provides a tasty enhancement.

1¼ cups boiling water
½ cup chopped fresh basil
2 large carrots (about 10 ounces total), peeled and thinly sliced lengthwise
1 large zucchini (about 12 ounces), sliced into paper-thin rounds
Salt and freshly ground black pepper, to taste
6 large portobello mushrooms (about 6 ounces), thoroughly cleaned, stems snapped off

2 plum tomatoes (about 6 ounces total), sliced into rounds
6 ounces thin asparagus, cut into 3-inch spears
1 large red bell pepper (about 10 ounces), seeded and sliced
1 small eggplant (about 10 ounces), thinly sliced
4 teaspoons unflavored gelatin (2 packets)

Mix the boiling water with the basil and set aside.

Line a 9¼-inch loaf pan with plastic wrap, leaving enough overlap to seal the terrine after the pan has been filled.

Bring a pot of water to a boil. Blanch the carrots for 2 minutes in boiling water, transfer them to a colander, rinse with cold water, and drain on paper toweling. While the carrots are draining, blanch the zucchini for 15 seconds, rinse, and drain.

Place the carrots lengthwise on the bottom of the plastic-lined loaf pan, then stand any remaining slices upright along all the sides, allowing the strips to drape over the sides of the pan. Reserve any leftover slices. Layer the zucchini over the carrot, overlapping rounds in a fish scale pattern. Dust with salt and pepper.

Blanch the mushrooms for 10 seconds, and drain. Dump the water from the pot, refill, and bring to a boil. Salt and pepper both sides of the mushrooms lightly, then layer them in the pan over the zucchini, cutting the mushrooms as needed to fit.

Next, add a layer of sliced tomatoes; dust with salt and pepper.

When the fresh water has come to a boil, add the asparagus

spears and blanch for 15 seconds. Rinse and drain. Layer the spears lengthwise to cover the tomatoes and dust them with salt and pepper.

Blanch the red pepper strips for 30 seconds, rinse, drain, and layer over the asparagus.

Blanch the eggplant for 30 seconds, rinse, drain, and layer on top.

Put the basil water in a small saucepan and place over medium heat just until the liquid begins to give off steam. Add the gelatin, reduce the heat to low, and stir with a wooden spoon until the gelatin is completely dissolved and the mixture begins to thicken. Pour over the vegetables in the loaf pan.

Fold the overhanging carrot strips over the top and add any that were reserved from the first step of assembly. Don't worry about any gaps or irregularities on the surface, as this will be the bottom of the finished terrine. Close the plastic wrap over the pan and top with an additional layer of doubled plastic wrap to seal.

Put the loaf pan onto a large plate and weigh the pan down with another loaf pan of the same size filled with water, bags of dried beans, or anything else sufficiently heavy, or with a brick. Refrigerate for at least 3 hours to allow the basil aspic to form and the terrine to set.

To unmold, open the plastic wrap, put a serving plate upside down on top of the loaf pan, flip, and remove the plastic. Cut into 8 slices.

*Yield—8 servings*
*Fat per serving—0.35 g.*

# Potato Cakes with Roasted Red Pepper Cream

**POTATO CAKES:**

4 cups peeled, cubed new red potatoes
  (about 1½ pounds)
1 tablespoon trimmed and chopped
  scallion (about 1 scallion)
¼ cup nonfat liquid egg substitute
1 teaspoon finely grated lemon rind
¼ cup nonfat sour cream
⅛ teaspoon coarse kosher salt
⅛ teaspoon white pepper

**ROASTED RED PEPPER CREAM:**

One 8-ounce red bell pepper, halved
  and seeded
½ cup buttermilk
¼ teaspoon salt
⅛ teaspoon white pepper

To make the cakes, put the potatoes in a 3-quart saucepan with water to cover. Bring to a boil over high heat and continue to boil for about 20 minutes, until the potatoes are fork tender.

Drain well, transfer to a large mixing bowl, and mash. Set aside and allow to cool completely to room temperature.

When the potatoes have cooled, add the remaining ingredients for the cakes. Mix well. Form into 12 cakes, using about a tablespoon of the mixture for each cake. Place the cakes on a nonstick baking sheet, cover with plastic wrap, and refrigerate for at least 1 hour.

For the cream, about 30 minutes before you want to serve, preheat the broiler and line the rack with aluminum foil.

Place the bell pepper on the rack, cut side down, 2 to 3 inches from the heat source. Broil for about 5 minutes, until charred. Remove the pepper and turn the oven down to 500 degrees.

Carefully transfer the pepper to an airtight plastic bag, seal, and let cool for about 10 minutes.

Remove the pepper from the plastic bag and rub off the skin. Put the pepper into a food processor or blender and puree to a smooth consistency while pouring in ¼ cup of the buttermilk. Set aside.

Remove the baking sheet from the refrigerator, uncover, and put in the oven. Bake for about 15 minutes, until the potato cakes are browned.

When the cakes are almost done, transfer the pepper puree to a small saucepan over low heat. Whisk in the remaining ¼ cup of buttermilk, the salt and white pepper. Cook for 1 minute more to heat thoroughly.

Serve 2 cakes per person, browned side up, and surround with red pepper cream.

*Yield—6 servings*
*Fat per serving—0.33 g.*

# Pumpkin Ravioli

This subtle yet sophisticated first course proves just how far fat-free cooking has come since the days of cottage cheese and crackers. Our crescent-shaped pies are actually lunettes, rather than the more traditional square ravioli. The sweet apple and carrot sauce requires a juice extractor. If you don't have one, try the Caramelized Onion and Roasted Tomato Sauce (page 23) from our Zucchini Ravioli.

*DOUGH:*
2 cups all-purpose flour, plus a little extra
    for flouring during preparation
⅔ cup nonfat liquid egg substitute

*FILLING:*
½ cup pumpkin puree
1 tablespoon nonfat liquid egg substitute
1 teaspoon ground cumin

*ASSEMBLY:*
1 tablespoon nonfat liquid egg substitute

*SAUCE:*
2 MacIntosh apples (about 10 ounces
    total), quartered
2 large carrots (about 10 ounces total)
2 teaspoons cornstarch
4 teaspoons water
Chopped fresh parsley, for garnish

To make the dough, put the flour into the bowl of a food processor and pulse while adding the egg substitute. This will produce bits of dough about the size of large peas.

Turn out onto a floured board and knead the dough into a single ball that is glossy and elastic. Enclose in plastic wrap and set aside for 30 minutes.

While the dough is resting, mix all the filling ingredients together well. Set aside.

Flour the rollers of a pasta machine. Cut the dough in half, flour all over, and flatten. Put the first piece of dough through the largest opening on the pasta machine 3 times, folding it in half after each time through. Then put it through each successively smaller opening, until it has gone through the smallest. Repeat with the second piece of dough.

From each thin piece of dough, cut twelve 3-inch circles. Put 1 teaspoon of filling in the center of each circle. Paint the exposed dough with egg substitute (1 tablespoon should suffice to paint all 24 circles). Fold each circle in half to form a crescent-shaped ravioli and crimp the edges together to seal.

For the sauce, run the apples and carrots through a juice extractor. You should have about 1 cup of juice.

In a small bowl, combine the cornstarch and water.

Put the juice in a small saucepan and cook over medium heat just until the liquid begins to give off steam, about 2 minutes. Remove from the heat, whisk in the cornstarch mixture, return to heat, and cook for 2 minutes more. Reduce the heat to very low to keep warm while the ravioli cook.

Bring a large saucepan of water to a boil. Drop in the ravioli and cook over medium heat for about 5 minutes. When the ravioli rise to the surface of the boiling water, they are done.

Serve 3 ravioli per portion, topped with some of the apple-carrot sauce and a sprinkling of parsley.

*Yield — 8 servings*
*Fat per serving — 0.47 g*

# Peppered Potatoes

1 pound small unpeeled new red potatoes        ½ cup peppered vodka
     (about 10 potatoes), quartered

Fill the bottom of a steamer with water and bring to a boil. Put the potatoes into the steamer basket, cover, and steam for 8 to 10 minutes, until fork tender. Remove from the heat and drain the potatoes.

Transfer to a bowl. Pour the vodka over the potatoes and toss a minute or two to allow the vodka to be absorbed.

*Yield — 10 servings*
*Fat per serving — 0.03 g.*

# 3

# SOUPS

# Roasted Acorn Squash Soup with Maple Cream

1 acorn squash (about 1½ pounds)
1 cup chopped celery (about 2 stalks)
⅔ cup peeled, chopped carrot
   (about 1 carrot)
1¼ cups coarsely chopped yellow onion
   (about 1 onion)
2 cups 99% Fat-Free Chicken Stock
   (page 10)

¼ teaspoon ground nutmeg
Up to ⅛ teaspoon cayenne pepper, to taste
½ cup Yogurt Cheese (see Pantry)
¼ cup pure maple syrup
1 tablespoon trimmed and finely chopped
   scallion (about 1 scallion), for garnish

Preheat the oven to 350 degrees.

Cut the squash in half, scoop out and discard the seeds. Place, cut side down, on a foil-lined baking sheet. Bake for about 45 minutes, until the squash is fork tender. Let cool a bit, then peel.

Combine the celery, carrot, and onion in a heavy saucepan. Cover and cook for about 10 minutes over low heat, until the onion has wilted. Add the chicken stock and bring to a boil over medium heat. Lower the heat, cover, and simmer for 20 minutes.

Puree the soup mixture with the squash in a food processor or blender until smooth. Return to the pan, add the spices, and cook for 3 minutes more, until thoroughly heated.

Meanwhile, combine the yogurt cheese and maple syrup.

Top each bowl of soup with about 1½ tablespoons maple cream and a sprinkling of scallion.

*Yield—4 servings*
*Fat per serving—0.55 g.*

Oven-roasting the acorn squash intensifies its sweet, nutty taste. Using yogurt cheese as a base lends the maple cream enough body to garnish this rich soup.

# Creamy Leek Soup

Pureed potato gives this soup the thick, creamy texture normally provided by dairy products.

5 cups trimmed, sliced leek, white and light green parts only (about 1 pound)
2½ cups peeled, cubed red potatoes (about 1 pound)

4 cups 99% Fat-Free Chicken Stock (page 10)
Chopped fresh chives, for garnish

Combine all the ingredients except the chives in a large saucepan and bring to a boil. Lower the heat, cover, and simmer for 1 hour.

Transfer to a food processor or blender and puree. Return the soup to the pan and reheat for 3 minutes.

Garnish with the chopped fresh chives and serve immediately.

*Yield — 6 servings*
*Fat per serving — 0.16 g.*

# Winter Vegetable Soup

1 cup trimmed and sliced leek, white and
    light green parts only (3–4 ounces)
1½ cups thinly sliced yellow onion
    (about 1 onion)
2 teaspoons chopped garlic
    (about 3 cloves)
1 cup chopped celery (2–3 stalks)
1½ cups peeled, chopped carrots
    (about 3 carrots)
1½ cups peeled, chopped parsnips
    (about 2 parsnips)
1 cup peeled, finely chopped red potato
    (about 1 medium potato)

1 bay leaf
2 tablespoons chopped flat-leaf parsley
2 teaspoons dried basil
½ teaspoon ground sage
⅛ teaspoon cayenne pepper
7 cups water
2 cups shredded savoy cabbage
    (about 8 ounces)
15½ ounces canned butter beans, drained
    and rinsed
1 cup peeled, seeded, and chopped fresh
    tomatoes (about 2 tomatoes)

Combine the leek, onion, garlic, celery, and carrots in a nonstick stockpot. Cook for about 20 minutes over low heat, stirring occasionally, until the vegetables look dry.

Add the parsnips and potato. Mix in the bay leaf, parsley, basil, sage, and cayenne pepper. Add the water. Bring to a boil, lower the heat, cover partially, and simmer for 40 minutes.

Stir in the cabbage and cook for another 5 minutes. Remove the bay leaf. Transfer 1 cup of liquid from the stockpot to a food processor or blender, add the beans, and puree. Stir back into the stock. Raise the heat to medium, bring to a boil, and cook for 10 minutes. Add the tomatoes and cook for an additional 2 to 3 minutes.

*Yield — 8 servings (6 as a main course)*
*Fat per serving — 0.42 g. (0.56 g. for main course)*

Our version of the classic minestrone. Instead of floating butter beans in the soup, we puree them for use as a thickening agent in lieu of butter and flour.

# Tortilla Soup

*We* broil the tortilla chips to obtain the crispness usually achieved by frying.

*Six 6-inch corn tortillas*
*3 cups 99% Fat-Free Chicken Stock*
  *(page 10)*
*1 tablespoon freshly squeezed lime juice*
*⅛ teaspoon ground cumin*
*¼ teaspoon ground turmeric*
*Dash each of salt and cayenne pepper,*
  *to taste*

*½ cup corn kernels (about 1 ear)*
*3 tablespoons chopped fresh cilantro*
*3 tablespoons seeded, very finely chopped*
  *fresh jalapeño pepper (about 1 large*
  *pepper), for garnish (optional)*

Preheat the broiler.

Cut the tortillas into long, ½-inch-wide strips. Place them under the broiler until crisp, about 1 minute per side, taking care not to burn them. Remove from the oven and set aside.

Combine the chicken stock, lime juice, and spices in a saucepan and cook for 10 minutes over medium heat.

Divide the toasted tortilla strips, corn kernels, and cilantro among 6 small bowls, and pour the hot soup on top. Garnish, if desired, with the chopped jalapeño pepper. Serve immediately.

*Yield—6 servings*
*Fat per serving—0.21 g.*

# Cucumber Soup

4 cups peeled, coarsely chopped cucumber
   (about two 1-pound cucumbers)
½ teaspoon salt
¼ cup champagne vinegar
1½ cups 99% Fat-Free Chicken Stock
   (page 10)

¼ cup dry vermouth
¼ teaspoon white pepper
½ cup chopped fresh dill weed, plus
   additional for garnish
About 6 tablespoons plain nonfat yogurt,
   for garnish

Combine the cucumber and salt in a nonreactive bowl and toss to coat the cucumber well. Set aside for about 30 minutes.

Rinse the cucumber under cold running water for about 1 minute, shake off the excess water, and pat dry. Transfer to a food processor or blender, add the vinegar, and puree to a smooth consistency.

Combine the chicken stock, vermouth, and pepper in a medium saucepan. Bring to a boil over medium heat. Whisk in the cucumber puree and the chopped dill and cook for another 2 minutes, stirring occasionally.

Ladle into 6 soup bowls and garnish each serving with a dollop of yogurt and a sprinkling of fresh dill.

*Yield—6 servings*
*Fat per serving—0.20 g.*

Whereas most cucumber soups are cold summertime fare, this version is served warm year-round.

# Cream of Pumpkin Soup

1 cup chopped white onion (about
   1 medium onion)
3 tablespoons water
½ teaspoon freshly grated ginger
¼ teaspoon coarse kosher salt
¼ teaspoon curry powder
⅛ teaspoon freshly ground black pepper

1 cup pumpkin puree
1 cup 99% Fat-Free Chicken Stock
   (page 10)
½ cup skim milk
½ cup evaporated skim milk
Snipped fresh chives, for garnish

Put the onion and water in a saucepan over low heat. Cook for about 12 minutes, until all the water has evaporated and the onion is tender.

Remove from the heat and stir in the seasonings, mixing until the onion is coated. Add the pumpkin and mix until well incorporated. Stir in the stock and skim milk until blended.

Return to medium heat and bring to a boil, stirring constantly. Lower the heat and simmer, uncovered, for 10 minutes. Stir in the evaporated milk and cook for another 4 minutes.

Ladle into 4 small soup bowls, garnish with chives, and serve.

*Yield—4 servings*
*Fat per serving—0.18 g.*

# Cream of Garlic Soup

2 cups 99% Fat-Free Chicken Stock
   (page 10)
10 cloves garlic (about 2 ounces)
⅔ cup peeled, diced red potato (about 1
   small potato)
½ cup trimmed, sliced leek, white and light
   green parts only (about 1½ ounces)

¼ cup plain nonfat yogurt
⅛ teaspoon white pepper
¼ teaspoon salt
Snipped fresh chives, for garnish

Combine the stock, garlic, potato, and leek in a saucepan and bring to a boil. Lower the heat and simmer for about 25 minutes, uncovered, until the vegetables are tender.

Strain the mixture through a sieve, reserving the liquid. Put the solids in the bowl of a food processor or blender, add ½ cup of the liquid, and puree.

Return the puree and the remainder of the reserved liquid to the saucepan and set over low heat. Whisk in the yogurt, salt, and pepper. Cook for another 2 minutes while whisking, until the soup begins to steam.

Put about a teaspoon of chives into each of 4 small bowls and pour the soup over.

*Yield—4 servings*
*Fat per serving—0.34 g.*

Pungent, intense, and aromatic—for garlic lovers only!

# Yellow Split-Pea Soup

This soup provides a truly hearty antidote to winter chills. Using smoked turkey stock supplies the nuance of ham without the fat.

2 medium white onions (about 14 ounces total), cut into 1-inch cubes
1 tablespoon chopped garlic (3–4 cloves)
2 cups yellow split peas (about 1 pound)
1 teaspoon dried oregano
½ teaspoon dried thyme
1 teaspoon salt
1 teaspoon freshly ground black pepper
⅛ teaspoon hot sauce
2 cups 99% Fat-Free Smoked Turkey Stock (page 8)
4 cups 99% Fat-Free Chicken Stock (page 10)

Put the onion in a large nonstick saucepan over medium-low heat. Cook for about 5 minutes, stirring constantly, until the onion is wilted and translucent. Add the garlic, stir, and continue to cook for 1 minute.

Stir in the split peas, then the seasonings, hot sauce, and stocks. Raise the heat to medium and bring to a boil. Reduce the heat to low, cover, and simmer for about 1 hour, until the soup is fairly thick. Remove the cover and stir well before serving.

*Yield — 6 servings*
*Fat per serving — 0.84 g.*

# Asparagus Soup

⅔ cup chopped yellow onion (about 1 small onion)

⅓ cup chopped shallot (about 2 shallots)

2 tablespoons water

3½ cups chopped asparagus tips (about 1 pound)

4 cups 99% Fat-Free Chicken Stock (page 10)

1 cup shredded spinach leaves, packed (about 2 ounces)

2 teaspoons chopped fresh tarragon

⅛ teaspoon freshly grated nutmeg, plus a dash for garnish

½ teaspoon salt

¼ teaspoon freshly ground black pepper

Combine the onion, shallot, and water in a nonstick frying pan. Cook for about 6 minutes over medium heat, stirring constantly, until onions are wilted. Stir in the asparagus and cook, stirring, for 1 minute more.

Add the stock and bring to a boil. Cover, lower heat, and simmer until the onion and asparagus are tender, about 30 minutes.

Transfer the contents of the pan to a food processor or blender. Add the spinach and tarragon, and puree until smooth. Add the nutmeg and process to blend. Return the mixture to the pan, add the salt and pepper, and reheat for about 3 minutes.

Garnish each serving with a small scraping of nutmeg.

*Yield — 6 servings*
*Fat per serving — 0.34 g.*

# Cream of Broccoli Soup

1 pound broccoli flowerets and tender
    stems (about 1 head)
2½ cups peeled, cubed small red potatoes
    (about 1 pound)
1 cup trimmed and chopped celery
    (about 2 stalks)
1 cup chopped yellow onion
    (about 1 onion)

2 cloves garlic, quartered
4 cups 99% Fat-Free Chicken Stock
    (page 10)
½ tablespoon chopped fresh tarragon
Chopped fresh chives, for garnish
Grated lemon rind, for garnish

Combine the broccoli, potatoes, celery, onion, garlic, and chicken stock in a 4-quart saucepan or pot over medium heat. Add the tarragon and bring to a boil. Lower the heat, cover, and simmer for 45 minutes.

Transfer the contents of the pot to a food processor or blender and puree. Return the soup to the pot and reheat for 3 minutes.

Garnish each serving lightly with chives and lemon rind.

*Yield—6 servings*
*Fat per serving—0.27 g.*

# Curried Chicken and Rice Soup

2 cups 99% Fat-Free Chicken Stock (page 10) or bouillon
1½ cups water
5 ounces skinless, boneless chicken breast, trimmed of all fat
½ cup finely chopped white onion (about 1 small onion)
2 large carrots (about 10 ounces total), peeled, trimmed, and cut into ½-inch chunks
2 stalks celery (about 4 ounces total), trimmed and cut into ½-inch chunks
¾ teaspoon curry powder
⅛ teaspoon freshly ground black pepper
¼ teaspoon coarse kosher salt
⅛ teaspoon ground cardamom
⅓ cup uncooked long-grain white rice
1 large fresh tomato (about 8 ounces), peeled, seeded, and chunked

Combine the chicken stock and water in a saucepan over medium heat and bring to a boil. Add the chicken breast and allow to come back to a boil. Lower the heat, cover, and simmer for about 15 minutes, until the chicken is fork tender. Remove and reserve the chicken. Stir in the onion, carrots, celery, and seasonings.

Rinse the rice under cold running water and drain.

Cut the chicken into small chunks. (You should have about ½ cup chunked chicken.)

Add the rice, chicken, and tomato to the saucepan, raise the heat to medium, and bring to a boil. Lower the heat, cover, and simmer for another 15 minutes.

*Yield — 6 servings*
*Fat per serving — 0.75 g.*

*Bouillon can be substituted in this recipe for the richer chicken stock, since we add flavor by precooking the chicken in the base. Make sure to trim all fat from the chicken breast.*

# Cranberry Soup

The blend of celery root and orange adds character to this surprisingly mellow cold soup, which has none of the tartness usually associated with cranberries.

1 cup cranberries (about 4 ounces)
½ cup peeled, trimmed, and grated celery root (about 2 ounces)
1 cup water

1½ cups freshly squeezed orange juice
2 tablespoons sugar
⅛ teaspoon ground sage
1 tablespoon port wine

Put the cranberries, celery root, and ½ cup of the water in a saucepan. Cook for about 10 minutes over medium-low heat, until all the cranberries have burst and are soft enough to mash.

Puree the mixture in a food processor or blender and return the puree to the pan.

Add the remaining ½ cup of water, the orange juice, sugar, and sage. Whisk well and cook over low heat for 10 minutes, uncovered. Add the port, and cook for 2 minutes longer.

Cover and refrigerate the soup for at least 2 hours, until thoroughly chilled.

Yield—4 servings
Fat per serving—0.30 g.

# Minted Melon Soup

6 cups peeled, seeded, and cubed honeydew
   melon (about one 4-pound melon)
¼ cup freshly squeezed lemon juice
   (about 1 lemon)
2 cups plain nonfat yogurt, plus
   additional for garnish

¼ cup chopped fresh mint, tightly packed,
   plus 6 whole sprigs for garnish
1 cup peeled, chopped cucumber
   (about 1 large cucumber)

Combine the melon, lemon juice, yogurt, and chopped mint in a food processor or blender and puree. Cover and refrigerate for at least 2 hours, until thoroughly chilled.

Stir the cucumber into the puree and serve in small chilled bowls, garnished with a sprig of mint and a little yogurt.

Yield—6 servings
Fat per serving—0.29 g.

A deceptively simple recipe with a delightfully complex result.

# Pear Port Soup

A refreshing and sweet summertime repast. The long simmering takes the edge off the wine, leaving only its distinctive flavor. The better the wine used in this recipe, the better the soup.

8 cups peeled, cored, and chopped ripe
   Anjou pears (about 3 pounds)
1 cup sugar

5 cups tawny port wine
1½ cups water

Combine all the ingredients in a saucepan and simmer for 45 minutes, uncovered, until the pears are tender enough to be easily mashed with a wooden spoon.

Puree in a food processor or blender and chill for at least 2 hours before serving.

Yield — 6 servings
Fat per serving — 0.85 g.

# Carrot Soup

6 cups peeled, trimmed, and shredded
  carrots (about 2 pounds)
⅔ cup peeled, finely diced red potato
  (about 1 small potato)
½ cup grated white onion
  (about 1 small onion)
½ teaspoon coarse kosher salt
1 teaspoon chopped fresh thyme

1 tablespoon chopped fresh dillweed, plus
  additional for garnish
4 cups water
1 clove garlic
½ cup plain nonfat yogurt, plus additional
  for garnish
½ cup buttermilk

Combine the carrots, potato, onion, salt, thyme, dillweed, and water in a saucepan. Press in the garlic and bring to a boil over
medium heat. Lower the heat and simmer for 20 minutes, uncovered.

Puree the mixture in a food processor or blender. Transfer to a
bowl and whisk in the yogurt and buttermilk. Cover and refrigerate
for at least 2 hours, until well chilled.

Garnish each serving with a little yogurt and dill.

Yield—6 servings
Fat per serving—0.41 g.

# Watercress Vichyssoise

The marriage of two distinguished cold soups. Our version uses yogurt in place of the traditional heavy cream and butter.

2 cups stemmed, chopped watercress, plus
   6 whole sprigs for garnish
   (about 12 ounces total)
4 cups peeled, finely cubed red potatoes
   (about 1½ pounds)
2½ cups skim milk
1 teaspoon coarse kosher salt

¼ teaspoon white pepper
½ cup chopped white onion
2 cups peeled, chopped cucumber (about
   one 1-pound cucumber)
¾ cup plain nonfat yogurt, plus additional
   for garnish

Combine the chopped watercress, potatoes, milk, salt, white pepper, and onion in a saucepan. Bring to a boil over medium heat, lower the heat, and simmer for 20 minutes, uncovered.

Transfer to a food processor or blender and puree while adding the cucumber. Transfer the puree to a bowl, whisk in the yogurt, and cover. Refrigerate for at least 2 hours, until very well chilled.

Garnish each serving with a sprig of watercress and, if desired, a dollop yogurt.

*Yield—6 servings*
*Fat per serving—0.45 g.*

# Cantaloupe Soup

3⅓ cups peeled, seeded, and cubed cantaloupe (about one 2½-pound melon)
¾ cup apricot nectar

2 teaspoons grated lemon rind
4 teaspoons freshly squeezed lemon juice
½ teaspoon ground clove
4 sprigs fresh mint, for garnish

Combine the melon, nectar, and lemon rind in a food processor or blender and puree. Transfer to a mixing bowl and whisk in the lemon juice and clove. Cover and chill in the refrigerator for at least 2 hours before serving.

Garnish each serving with a sprig of fresh mint.

*Yield—4 servings*
*Fat per serving—0.39 g.*

# Roasted Beet and Red Pepper Borscht

This is a new twist on an old favorite. The addition of roasted pepper and ginger creates a taste that is as vibrant and intense as its color. We use baby beets and then roast them to capitalize on their intrinsic sweetness.

*1 pound whole baby beets, trimmed*
*One 4-ounce red bell pepper*
*4 teaspoons freshly grated ginger*
*2 cups water*
*4 teaspoons freshly squeezed lemon juice*

*2 teaspoons sugar*
*1⅓ cups plain nonfat yogurt, plus additional for garnish*
*Chopped fresh chives, for garnish*

Preheat the oven to 375 degrees.

Wrap the beets in aluminum foil and roast them for about 45 minutes, until just tender when pierced with a wooden skewer. Remove from the oven, unwrap, and set aside.

Turn the oven up to preheat the broiler and line the rack with aluminum foil. Cut the bell pepper in half lengthwise, core, and seed. Place on the rack, cut side down, 2 to 3 inches from the heat source. Broil for about 5 minutes, until charred. Remove the pepper carefully with tongs and seal in an airtight plastic bag. Let cool for about 10 minutes.

Peel the beets and cut them into cubes. (You should have about 1 cup cubed beets.) Transfer the cubes to a saucepan.

Remove the pepper from the plastic bag, rub off the skin, and chop. (This should render about ¼ cup.) Add to the beets. Add the ginger and water. Bring to a boil over medium heat, lower the heat to a bare simmer, and cook for 10 minutes uncovered.

Puree the soup in a food processor or blender for 1 minute, then transfer it to a mixing bowl. Whisk in the lemon juice, sugar, and yogurt. Cover and refrigerate for at least 2 hours to chill.

Garnish each serving with a dollop of yogurt and a sprinkling of chives.

*Yield—4 servings*
*Fat per serving—0.17 g.*

# Roasted Vegetable Soup

3 medium yellow onions (about 1
    pound total), quartered
1 whole, unpeeled head garlic, top trimmed
1 pound unpeeled banana squash, cut
    into large chunks

1 sprig fresh thyme (optional)
2⅔ cups 99% Fat-Free Chicken Stock
    (page 10)
½ cup water
1 cup evaporated skim milk

Preheat the oven to 300 degrees.

Put the onions, garlic, squash, and thyme into a glass baking dish. Add 1 cup of the chicken stock and bake, uncovered, for 1½ hours.

Remove the dish from the oven and allow to cool for about 1 hour.

Remove the squash from the baking dish, peel, and place in the bowl of a blender. Add the onion. Separate the garlic cloves and squeeze the meats from their peels into the blender. Pour in the cooking stock. Add the water to the emptied baking dish, swirl to combine with any residual stock, and add to the ingredients in the blender. Puree to a smooth consistency. (This should yield about 2½ cups of puree.)

Transfer the puree to a large saucepan or stockpot. Stir in the remaining 1⅔ cups of chicken stock and the evaporated milk. Cook over medium heat for 5 minutes. Serve immediately.

*Yield—6 servings*
*Fat per serving—0.43 g.*

# 4

# SALADS

# Ann's Hash Brown Potato Salad

1 pound unpeeled new red potatoes
Light vegetable oil cooking spray
½ teaspoon mustard seed
¼ cup cider vinegar
½ cup diced red onion
½ cup plain nonfat yogurt

1 teaspoon Dijon mustard
¼ cup chopped flat-leaf parsley
2 teaspoons finely chopped fresh rosemary
¼ teaspoon freshly ground black pepper
1 cup halved red cherry tomatoes
  (about ½ pound tomatoes)

Preheat the oven to 350 degrees.

Fill the bottom of a steamer with water and bring to a boil. Place the potatoes in the steamer basket, cover, and steam for about 10 minutes, until fork tender. Cool for about 5 minutes and cut into ¼-inch-thick slices.

Spray a cookie or baking sheet twice lightly with the vegetable oil spray and distribute the oil evenly over the surface. Place the potato slices on the sheet in a single layer. Bake for about 15 minutes, turning the slices after 8 minutes, until golden brown. Remove from the oven and set aside.

Put the mustard seed into a cast-iron frying pan, covered, over high heat. As soon as the seeds begin to pop (like popcorn), add the vinegar, re-cover, and remove from the heat.

Combine the onion, yogurt, Dijon mustard, parsley, rosemary, and pepper in a large serving bowl. Mix well. Stir in the popped mustard seed. Add the potato slices, then the tomatoes, tossing to coat.

*Yield—6 servings*
*Fat per serving—0.78 g.*

We named this salad for our talented friend Ann Bloomstrand, whose thoughtful suggestions and critical palate helped shape our salad-making endeavors.

# Roasted Eggplant Pasta Salad

This stylized treatment of pasta salad orchestrates the intense but complementary tastes of roasted eggplant, roasted zucchini, and roasted pepper.

2 Chinese eggplants (about 1 pound total), cut into ¼-inch rounds
2 teaspoons coarse kosher salt
Light vegetable oil cooking spray
4 small zucchini (about 1 pound total), cut into ¼-inch rounds
One 4-ounce red bell pepper
1 cup cooked pasta (see Pantry)
2 tablespoons diced green bell pepper
2 tablespoons trimmed and chopped scallion (about 2 scallions)
2 tablespoons chopped fresh curly-leaf parsley

DRESSING:
½ cup plain nonfat yogurt
1 clove garlic
2 tablespoons chopped fresh basil

Put the eggplant in a colander. Sprinkle with the salt, and toss to coat. Set aside for 30 minutes. Rinse the eggplant and pat dry.

Meanwhile, preheat the oven to 350 degrees.

Spray a nonstick baking sheet twice lightly with the vegetable oil spray and smooth the oil evenly the over surface. Spread the eggplant and zucchini slices on the sheet in a single layer. Spray twice lightly over the vegetables with the vegetable oil spray. Bake for 25 to 30 minutes, turning the slices after 10 minutes, until golden brown.

Remove from the oven and turn the heat up to broil. Line the broiler rack with aluminum foil.

Cut the red bell pepper in half lengthwise, core, and seed.

Place it on the rack, cut side down, 2 to 3 inches from the heat source. Broil for about 5 minutes, until charred. Remove carefully and seal in an airtight plastic bag. Let cool for about 10 minutes.

Remove from the plastic bag, rub off the skin, and chop the pepper. (This should render about ¼ cup chopped pepper.)

Combine the eggplant, zucchini, roasted red pepper, pasta, green pepper, scallion, and parsley in a large serving bowl and mix well.

For the dressing, press the garlic into the yogurt. Stir in the basil. Pour over the pasta salad and toss well to coat.

*Yield — 6 servings*
*Fat per serving — 0.98 g.*

# Papaya and Watercress Salad

A cool and refreshing last-course salad to follow a spicy entrée, this is also visually stunning, with a fan of papaya emerging from a base of watercress on the plate.

One 1-pound papaya, peeled, seeded, and
    cut lengthwise into thin slices
4 ounces watercress, trimmed

⅓ cup julienned red onion
¼ cup Honey-Ginger Dressing
    (page 187)

Fan an equal amount of papaya on each of 4 plates. Mound the watercress at the base of the fan and sprinkle the onion on top of the papaya. Use 1 tablespoon of dressing for each serving.

*Yield — 4 servings*
*Fat per serving — 0.14 g. (including dressing)*

# Composed Fruit Salad

4 niño (or finger) bananas (about 8
    ounces total)
1 tablespoon freshly squeezed lemon juice
8 ounces whole strawberries (do not hull)
2 cups trimmed, very thinly sliced spinach
    (about 4 ounces)
2 kiwis (about 8 ounces total), peeled
    and sliced

DRESSING:
2 tablespoons freshly squeezed lemon juice
½ teaspoon grated lemon rind
½ teaspoon poppy seed
¼ cup plain nonfat yogurt
4 teaspoons light corn syrup

Peel the bananas and cut them in half lengthwise. Combine with the 1 tablespoon lemon juice and mix to coat.

Partially slice the strawberries lengthwise to create fans.

To compose the salads, mound the spinach on the top half of each of 4 plates. Overlap kiwi slices on the lefthand side of the bottom half of the plate. Place the fanned strawberries on the righthand side, with 2 banana slices in the middle. Cover the plates with plastic wrap and refrigerate the salads for at least 1 hour before serving.

For the dressing, combine all the ingredients, whisk thoroughly, and drizzle over the salads.

*Yield—4 servings*
*Fat per serving—0.88 g.*

# Warm Cassoulet Salad

A light rendition of the traditional cassoulet, perfect for Sunday suppers or the buffet. All this needs is a loaf of crusty bread (try the French Country Round on page 134) and a bottle of good dry white wine.

1 cup thinly sliced white onion
  (about 1 medium onion)
5 tablespoons white wine
2 teaspoons finely chopped garlic
  (about 3 cloves)
4 ounces skinless smoked turkey breast,
  shredded
1 small head Napa cabbage (about
  1¼ pounds), thinly sliced

2 cups cooked Great Northern beans
1 cup 99% Fat-Free Smoked Turkey
  Stock (page 8)
1 teaspoon ground sage
½ teaspoon dried thyme
½ teaspoon salt

Combine the onion and 1 tablespoon of the wine in a saucepan and cook for about 3 minutes over low heat, until the onion is wilted. Add the garlic and cook for another minute.

Add the turkey, cabbage, beans, stock, spices, and the rest of the wine. Cover and cook for 2 minutes. Stir, and cook for about 2 minutes more, uncovered, until the cabbage begins to wilt. Serve warm.

*Yield—8 servings*
*Fat per serving—0.86 g.*

# Wild Rice Salad

1 cup cooked wild rice
¼ cup diced red bell pepper
2 large radishes, halved lengthwise and
    thinly sliced across (about ¼ cup slices)
1½ tablespoons trimmed, chopped scallion
    (about 1 scallion)

*DRESSING:*

½ tablespoon prepared white horseradish
½ tablespoon Dijon mustard
2 tablespoons white wine vinegar

Put the wild rice, bell pepper, radishes, and scallion in a salad bowl and mix together well.

For the dressing, combine all the ingredients in a small bowl and whisk thoroughly. Pour over the salad, toss, and serve.

*Yield — 4 servings*
*Fat per serving — 0.33 g.*

# Red and White Cabbage Slaw

We added the crunch of caraway to this colorful medley and took away the fatty mayonnaise dressing that drowns the typical coleslaw.

1 cup shredded red cabbage
1 cup shredded white cabbage
½ cup peeled, shredded carrot
   (about 1 carrot)
¼ cup finely chopped white onion
½ cup seeded, chopped yellow bell pepper
½ tablespoon caraway seed

DRESSING:
1 tablespoon stone-ground mustard
½ tablespoon freshly squeezed lemon juice
⅓ cup plain nonfat yogurt
¼ teaspoon sugar
¼ teaspoon salt

Combine the vegetables and caraway in a large serving bowl and mix well.

For the dressing, whisk the mustard and lemon juice together in a small bowl. Whisk in the yogurt, then the sugar and salt. Pour over the cabbage mixture and toss thoroughly.

Serve room temperature or chilled.

*Yield—4 servings*
*Fat per serving—0.55 g.*

# Diced Cucumber and Roasted Beet Salad

2 large beets (about 1 pound total)
1 cup peeled, seeded, and diced cucumber
½ cup diced red onion

*DRESSING:*
½ cup plain nonfat yogurt
3 tablespoons chopped fresh dill
1 tablespoon freshly squeezed lemon juice
½ teaspoon salt
¼ teaspoon white pepper

Preheat the oven to 350 degrees.

Wrap the beets securely in a double thickness of aluminum foil and roast in the oven for 1½ hours.

Remove from the oven, open the foil, and set aside for about 10 minutes to allow the beets to cool. Peel and dice the cooled beets.

Combine the diced beets, cucumber, and onion in a serving bowl.

For the dressing, whisk together the ingredients. Pour the dressing over the diced vegetables, and toss to coat thoroughly. Chill for at least 1 hour in the refrigerator before serving.

*Yield — 6 servings*
*Fat per serving — 0.12 g.*

Roasting the beets provides a novel twist to this traditional Swedish smorgasbord fare.

# Tossed Jicama and Snap-Pea Salad

4 ounces sugar snap peas, trimmed
½ pound romaine lettuce, torn into
    bite-sized pieces
4 ounces jicama, peeled and cut into
    matchstick slices (about ⅔ cup
    sliced jicama)

¼ cup julienned red onion
¼ cup Honey-Mustard Dressing
    (page 185)

Fill a saucepan at least halfway with water and bring to a boil. Blanch the peas by dropping them into the boiling water and immediately removing the pan from the heat. Drain and rinse at once under cold running water.

Combine the blanched peas, romaine lettuce, jicama, and onion in a serving bowl. Combine with the dressing, toss, and serve.

*Yield—4 servings*
*Fat per serving—0.58 g. (including dressing)*

# Black Bean Garden Salad

1 cup cooked black beans
½ cup husked, sliced tomatillos
    (about 2 tomatillos)
½ cup seeded, chopped red bell pepper
½ cup seeded, chopped yellow bell pepper
1 cup peeled, seeded, and cubed cucumber
    (about 1 medium cucumber)
½ medium red onion, sliced into half
    rounds (about 1 cup)
½ cup julienned jicama
1 cup seeded, chopped tomato (about
    1 large tomato)
1 cup chopped fresh cilantro
8 large leaves red-leaf lettuce, chilled
Snipped fresh chives, for garnish

*DRESSING:*

½ tablespoon Dijon mustard
1 tablespoon raspberry vinegar
¾ cup apricot nectar
½ teaspoon salt
½ teaspoon freshly ground black pepper
¼ teaspoon crushed red pepper flakes

Combine the black beans, vegetables, and cilantro in a large salad bowl and mix well.

For the dressing, whisk together the ingredients in a small bowl.

Pour the dressing over the salad and toss thoroughly. Cover and chill for at least 1 hour before serving. When you refrigerate the salad, also put 8 salad plates in to chill.

Line each plate with a chilled lettuce leaf, top with a serving of salad, and garnish with a bit of snipped chives.

*Yield — 8 servings*
*Fat per serving — 0.69 g.*

Vibrant sprays of colorful crisp vegetables permeate the salad bowl. This is a substantial salad that can also serve as a full summertime meal.

# Minted Fruit Salad

Refreshing mint and creamy sherried yogurt impart unexpected verve to this fruit salad. Pair it with a Pasta Frittata (page 90) to complete our update of the classic quiche and fruit plate.

8 ounces strawberries, hulled
3 ounces blueberries, picked over
One 3-ounce plum, pitted, thinly sliced
8 cantaloupe balls (about 4 ounces)
8 honeydew balls
1 teaspoon sugar
2 tablespoons freshly squeezed
   orange juice
1 tablespoon chopped fresh mint, plus
   additional for garnish

DRESSING:
½ cup nonfat vanilla yogurt
1 tablespoon sherry

Combine the fruit in a large mixing bowl. Add the sugar, orange juice, and mint. Mix to coat evenly.

For the dressing, whisk the sherry into the yogurt.

Distribute fruit salad among 4 individual serving bowls. Top each portion with 2 tablespoons of the sherried yogurt and garnish with chopped mint. Refrigerate for 1 hour to chill before serving.

*Yield—4 servings*
*Fat per serving—0.54 g.*

# Orange-Watercress Salad

16 leaves Belgian endive (about 8 ounces)
2 cups trimmed watercress
    (about 6 ounces)
2 navel oranges (about 1 pound total),
    peeled and cut into segments

⅓ cup pomegranate seeds (about 5 ounces)
6 tablespoons Orange-Honey Dressing
    (page 189)

To assemble the salads, fan 4 leaves of endive on each of 4 salad plates, with the bottom of the leaves meeting about two-thirds of the way down from the top of the plate. Mound ½ cup watercress at the juncture, and arrange 5 orange segments on the bottom third of the plate. Sprinkle the pomegranate seeds over each salad. Top each serving with 1½ tablespoons of the dressing.

*Yield — 4 servings*
*Fat per serving — 0.32 g. (including dressing)*

A smashing accompaniment to the Curried Lobster Risotto (page 106).

# Radish Sprout and Lentil Salad

The crunchy lentils provide a distinctive contrast, and the cool watercress a taming edge, to the pungent bite of radish sprouts in this salad.

1 cup dried lentils
3 cups water
1 shallot
1 clove garlic
1 bay leaf
1 cup radish sprouts
½ cup chopped watercress

DRESSING:
¼ cup freshly squeezed orange juice
1 teaspoon Dijon mustard
1 tablespoon white wine vinegar
⅛ teaspoon freshly ground black pepper
¼ teaspoon salt

Rinse, drain, and set aside the lentils.

Put the water and shallot in a saucepan over medium heat and bring to a boil. Add the garlic, bay leaf, and lentils. Reduce the heat and simmer for 15 minutes, uncovered. Do not overcook; the lentils should have a crunch. Drain the lentils, discarding the shallot, garlic, and bay leaf.

For the dressing, combine the ingredients in a small bowl and whisk to blend.

Mix the lentils, sprouts, and watercress in a salad bowl. Add the dressing and toss to combine. Cover and refrigerate the salad for 2 to 3 hours before serving.

*Yield — 6 servings*
*Fat per serving — 0.57 g.*

# Colin's Roasted Ginger-Beet Salad

2 large beets (about 1 pound total)
4 slices fresh ginger, each the size
   of a quarter
8 leaves green-leaf lettuce
2 ounces white flowering kale
2 navel oranges (about 1 pound total),
   peeled and cut into segments
2 tablespoons trimmed and chopped
   scallions (about 2 scallions)

*DRESSING:*
2 tablespoons freshly squeezed
   orange juice
¼ teaspoon freshly grated ginger
Dash of white pepper
¼ teaspoon light corn syrup

Preheat the oven to 350 degrees.

Wrap the beets and sliced ginger securely in a double thickness of aluminum foil. Roast in the oven for 1½ hours.

Remove the beets and turn up the oven to preheat the broiler (if you will be broiling rather than grilling the beets).

Open the foil and allow the beets to cool for 10 minutes. Discard the ginger, peel the beets, and cut them into ¼-inch slices. Grill or broil the beet slices for about 3 minutes per side, until browned.

Place 2 lettuce leaves in the upper left quarter of each salad plate. Place 2 medium-sized kale leaves in the upper right quarter. Overlap 3 roasted beet slices and 4 orange segments on the bottom half of the plate, sprinkling ½ tablespoon of scallion on top.

For the dressing, whisk together the ingredients in a small bowl and spoon the dressing evenly over the entire salad.

*Yield—4 servings*
*Fat per serving—0.38 g.*

Caterer and food consultant Colin Reeves lent his dramatic flair to the creation of this elegant composed salad, which juxtaposes dark roasted beets with white flowering kale.

# Grilled Potato Salad

For added texture,
we like to prepare the
potatoes on a stove-top
grill, but they can be
done in the broiler as
well.

1 red bell pepper (about 6 ounces)
1 pound new white potatoes
4 ounces arugula
¼ cup Mustard-Buttermilk Dressing
   (page 184)

4 teaspoons snipped fresh chives,
   for garnish

Preheat the broiler and line the rack with aluminum foil.

Halve, seed, and core the pepper. Broil, cut sides down, 2 to 3 inches from the heat source, for about 5 minutes, until charred. Remove carefully and seal in an airtight plastic bag to cool for about 10 minutes. Do not turn off the broiler. When cool, rub off the skin and cut the pepper into thin strips.

Meanwhile, fill the bottom of a steamer with water and bring to a boil. Put the potatoes into the steamer basket, cover, and steam for about 10 minutes, until fork tender.

Cut the potatoes into ¼-inch-thick slices, scatter them on a baking sheet, and grill or broil for about 2 minutes per side, until brown.

To compose the salads, cover the top half of each salad plate with arugula. On the bottom half, place a quarter of the potato slices. Lay strips of roasted pepper across the potato. Drizzle 1 tablespoon of dressing over the entire arrangement, and sprinkle about a teaspoon of chives on top.

*Yield—4 servings*
*Fat per serving—0.43 g. (including dressing)*

5

# *Main*
# COURSES

# Crab and Tomato Broth Couscous

1½ pounds plum tomatoes (about 10 tomatoes), cored and quartered
2 tablespoons chopped fresh basil
3 tablespoons chopped fresh flat-leaf parsley
1 tablespoon chopped fresh thyme

2 tablespoons chopped fresh tarragon
2 tablespoons chopped shallot
1 cup uncooked couscous
5 ounces uncooked crabmeat, cartilage and shells removed, rinsed

Puree the tomatoes in a food processor or blender.

Combine the pureed tomato, the basil, 2 tablespoons of the parsley, the thyme and tarragon in a small saucepan. Bring to a boil over medium heat and remove from the heat immediately. Work the puree through a food mill, producing a thin broth. Return it to the saucepan and bring to a simmer over low heat.

Preheat a cast-iron skillet over medium heat. Add the shallot and couscous. Cook for about 2 minutes over the medium heat, until the couscous is toasted. Stir in the hot tomato broth. Cook for about 2 minutes more, stirring constantly, until the broth has been absorbed.

Stir in the crabmeat, remove from the heat, and let sit for 2 minutes. Before serving, top with the remaining 1 tablespoon parsley.

*Yield—4 servings (6 servings as a first course)*
*Fat per serving—0.98 g. (0.65 g. as first course)*

Steeping the couscous in rich, mellow tomato broth enhances the flavor of this special dish and adds a rosy luster.

# Red Snapper and Black Bean Chili

No one will believe this rich snapper and black bean concoction has been prepared without the level of fat that usually sends chili off the meter! It took a long time to perfect this recipe, but we think it was worth the effort. The smoky taste is derived from adding a little bacon to the water below the basket in which the fish steams.

7¼ cups water
1½ cups dried black beans
1 small fresh poblano chile pepper (about 1½ ounces)
¾ cup finely chopped white onion (about 1 small onion)
¾ cup trimmed and finely chopped celery (about 2 stalks)
¾ cup peeled, finely chopped carrot (about 1 large carrot)
½ tablespoon chopped garlic (about 2 cloves)
2 tablespoons chopped fresh oregano
2 tablespoons chopped fresh thyme
1 bay leaf
2 teaspoons ground cumin

½ teaspoon freshly ground black pepper
One 28-ounce can peeled Italian-style plum tomatoes, with their juice
4 cups 99% Fat-Free Smoked Turkey Stock (page 8)
1 tablespoon red wine vinegar
½ teaspoon salt
¼ cup chopped fresh cilantro, plus additional for garnish
⅛ teaspoon cayenne pepper
2 tablespoons freshly squeezed lime juice (about 1 lime)
4 slices smoked bacon, cut into cubes (see Pantry)
7 ounces uncooked red snapper fillet
¼ teaspoon hot sauce (optional)

Preheat the broiler.

Bring 6 cups of the water to a boil in a 3-quart saucepan. Add the beans, bring back to a boil, and continue to boil for 5 minutes. Cover, remove from the heat, and let sit for 1 hour.

Broil the poblano chile, rotating it to char evenly on all sides, about 10 minutes. Remove from the oven and seal in an airtight plastic bag to cool for about 10 minutes. Then peel the pepper and remove the seeds, stem, and veins. Chop it fine and set aside.

Combine the onion, celery, carrot, garlic, and ¼ cup of the water in a large, heavy kettle or Dutch oven. Stir in the seasonings. Cover and cook for 7 minutes over low heat.

Meanwhile, drain the tomatoes, reserving the juice. Seed and coarsely chop the tomatoes, leaving a few large chunks intact.

Drain and rinse the beans. Stir into the kettle, along with the poblano, tomato and reserved juice, the turkey stock, vinegar, salt, and ½ cup of the water.

Raise the heat to medium and bring to a boil, then reduce the heat and simmer for 2½ hours, uncovered, stirring occasionally.

Stir in the cilantro, cayenne pepper, and the lime juice. Cover, turn off heat, and let sit to meld the flavors.

If preparing the chili a day in advance, cool it to room temperature, cover, and refrigerate. Remove from the refrigerator about 1 hour before serving and leave it at room temperature for 30 minutes before resuming the recipe.

Combine the bacon with enough water to fill the bottom of a steamer, but not enough to boil up through the holes into the steamer basket. Bring to a boil, put the snapper in the steamer basket, cover, and steam for 10 minutes. Remove and cool a bit. Peel the skin from the fish and cut the flesh into large bite-sized chunks.

Put the chili kettle back on medium-low heat. Stir in the remaining ½ cup of water and the optional hot sauce. Bring to a simmer and stir in the snapper. Cook for 5 minutes more. Garnish with cilantro if desired.

*Yield — 8 servings*
*Fat per serving — 0.99 g.*

# Chive Polenta with Mushroom Ragout

When we're lucky enough to find the extra-large variety of portobello mushrooms, we grill them to serve atop this dish.

*CHIVE POLENTA:*
2⅔ cups skim milk
⅓ cup buttermilk
1 teaspoon sugar
¼ teaspoon salt
1 cup yellow cornmeal
1 tablespoon snipped fresh chives

*MUSHROOM RAGOUT:*
2 tablespoons water
1 cup chopped white onion
  (about 1 medium onion)
½ tablespoon chopped garlic
  (about 2 cloves)
8 ounces shütake mushrooms, stemmed
  and chunked
8 ounces portobello mushrooms, stemmed
  and chunked
1 tablespoon dried oregano
1 tablespoon chopped fresh basil
½ cup dry white wine
One 28-ounce can peeled Italian-style
  plum tomatoes
½ teaspoon salt

For the polenta, combine the milks, sugar, and salt in a saucepan and bring to a simmer over medium heat. Slowly whisk in the cornmeal. Reduce the heat to low and continue to cook for about 5 minutes, stirring constantly with a wooden spoon, until the mixture is thick, smooth, and comes away easily from the sides of the pan. Remove from the heat and whisk in the chives. Pour into a 4-cup nonstick loaf pan, cover, and refrigerate for 1 hour.

Preheat the grill or broiler.

To make the ragout, put the water into a large, deep-sided non-stick frying pan over medium heat. Add the onion and garlic. Cook for about 4 minutes, stirring occasionally, until the onion is translucent. Reduce the heat slightly and add the mushrooms, oregano, basil, and ¼ cup of the wine. Stir, cover, and cook for 2 minutes.

Add the tomatoes, breaking them in half to release their juice, the remaining ¼ cup of wine, and the salt. Bring to a boil, lower the heat to a simmer, and cook, uncovered, for 20 minutes, stirring occasionally to prevent sticking.

Remove the polenta from the loaf pan and cut it into 12 slices. Grill or broil the slices for 2 to 3 minutes on each side, until brown, taking care not to burn them.

For each portion, serve about ⅔ cup of ragout atop 2 slices of toasted polenta.

*Yield—6 servings*
*Fat per serving—0.96 g.*

# Crab and Chicken Gumbo

This marvelously robust gumbo is derived from a dry, fat-free roux, which turns a rich, Cajun dark brown upon addition of the stock.

¼ cup all-purpose flour
2 strips smoked bacon, cut into cubes
   (see Pantry)
7 ounces skinless, boneless chicken breast
1 cup chopped white onion (about 1 onion)
½ cup seeded, chopped green bell pepper
½ cup seeded, chopped red bell pepper
¼ cup chopped celery
7 ounces okra, sliced into rounds
   (about ¾ cup)
½ tablespoon finely minced garlic
   (about 2 cloves)

1 bay leaf
¼ teaspoon freshly ground black pepper
⅛ teaspoon cayenne pepper
¼ teaspoon ground cumin
¼ teaspoon dried thyme
2 cups 99% Fat-Free Smoked Turkey
   Stock (page 8)
2 cups water
1 cup fresh crabmeat (about 5 ounces),
   cartilage and shell removed, rinsed
2½–3 cups cooked white rice
Chopped fresh parsley, for garnish

Put the flour into a small cast-iron or other heavy frying pan. Cook over medium heat, stirring constantly, for about 10 minutes, until the flour begins to turn an even dark tan. Take off the heat and remove the flour from the pan.

Fill the bottom of a steamer with enough water to cover, but not to boil up through the bottom of the steamer basket. Add the bacon and bring the water to a boil. If the chicken breast is whole, cut it into 3 or 4 pieces. When the water boils, put the chicken in the steamer basket, cover, and steam for 15 minutes. Remove the chicken and cut it into ½-inch cubes.

Combine the onion, peppers, celery, okra, and garlic in a heavy saucepan or Dutch oven. Cook for 5 minutes over medium-low heat, stirring constantly, until the vegetables become limp. Mix in all the seasonings. Stir in flour with a wooden spoon. While stirring, add the turkey stock and 2 cups water. Bring to a boil, reduce the heat to low, and throw in the chicken and crabmeat. Cover and simmer for 20 minutes.

Remove the bay leaf. Ladle about 1 cup of the gumbo into each bowl, adding about ½ cup tightly packed cooked rice to the center. (If serving as a soup course, use about ¾ cup gumbo topped with ⅓ cup rice.) Garnish with the parsley.

*Yield—6 servings (8 servings as soup course)*
*Fat per serving—0.95 g. (0.71 g. as soup course)*

This is elegant dinner-party fare. Spoon the coulis beneath or on top of the medallions, or compose the plate artistically. We like this accompanied by Steamed Bitter Greens (page 112).

# Turkey Medallions Stuffed with Mushroom Duxelle and Wild Rice on Cranberry-Orange Coulis

**TURKEY MEDALLIONS:**
2 cups finely chopped white button
    mushrooms (about ½ pound)
1 tablespoon freshly squeezed lemon juice
2 tablespoons water
⅛ teaspoon white pepper
1 teaspoon chopped fresh thyme
½ cup cooked wild rice
1 tablespoon skim milk
1 tablespoon nonfat cream cheese
Four uncooked 4-ounce slices skinless
    turkey breast

**CRANBERRY-ORANGE COULIS:**
1 medium navel orange (about 8 ounces),
    quartered and seeded
2 cups cranberries
½ cup orange juice
½ teaspoon sugar

Combine the mushrooms, lemon juice, and water in a saucepan. Simmer for 10 minutes over low heat, uncovered, stirring occasionally. Raise the heat to medium and boil until most of the liquid in the pan has evaporated, about 5 minutes. Whisk in the white pepper and thyme. Add the wild rice, milk, and cream cheese. Mix until thoroughly blended and remove from the heat.

Place each turkey slice between 2 sheets of wax paper approximately twice its size. Using a meat tenderizer, a rolling pin, or a rubber mallet, pound the turkey slices to about half their original thickness. Remove the top layer of wax paper.

On each slice, spread a quarter of the mushroom–wild rice filling, leaving a ¼-inch border all around. Lift a long edge and roll the turkey over onto itself into a cylinder. Tuck the ends under. Place the turkey roll on a square of aluminum foil, roll it closed, and twist the ends of the foil securely. Repeat this procedure for each of the remaining slices.

Fill a wide-bottomed sauté pan about halfway up with water and bring to a boil. Place the foil-encased turkey rolls into the boiling water and simmer, uncovered, for about 15 minutes over medium heat. The turkey rolls will be done when a metal cake tester or skewer inserted into the top of each roll comes out hot to the touch. Turn off heat and let the turkey rolls sit in the water.

For the coulis, combine the orange quarters with the cranberries in a food processor or blender and chop coarsely.

Transfer the mixture to a saucepan, add the orange juice, and bring to a boil over medium heat. Boil for 5 minutes, then add the sugar. Reduce the heat to low and simmer, uncovered, for about 15 minutes, until thick. Do not overcook.

Remove the turkey rolls from their foil wrappers and slice each on the diagonal into 6 medallions. Serve 4 medallions per person set on or around the coulis.

*Yield — 6 servings*
*Fat per serving — 0.97 g.*

# Turkey Moussaka in an Eggplant Boat

Although we use the more recognizable Greek name for this recipe, we have actually seasoned it in the style of the Turkish dish, *oturema*. Whereas the traditional preparation calls for beef or lamb, we have used turkey.

3 large baby eggplants (about 8 ounces each)
1½ teaspoons coarse kosher salt
1½ cups chopped yellow onion (about 1 large onion)
½ cup seeded, chopped green bell pepper
¼ cup water
12 ounces skinless turkey breast, ground (see Pantry)

1½ pounds peeled, diced fresh tomatoes (about 2 tomatoes)
2 teaspoons ground cinnamon
1 teaspoon ground allspice
1 tablespoon finely chopped dried apricot
½ cup chopped flat-leaf parsley

Slice the eggplants in half lengthwise. Sprinkle the cut sides with the coarse salt. Place in a colander, salted sides against the holes. Drain in the sink for 1 hour. Rinse and pat dry.

Preheat the broiler.

Place the eggplants in the broiler, cut sides up, about 5 inches from the heat source. Broil for 5 minutes, turn, and broil for about 8 minutes more on the skin side, until easily pierced with a fork. Remove and set aside.

Reset the oven to 400 degrees and allow it to cool.

Meanwhile, combine the onion, bell pepper, and water in a large nonstick frying pan. Cook over medium heat for about 6 minutes, stirring constantly, until the onion is translucent and the green pepper soft. Add the turkey and cook for about 5 minutes longer, stirring and crushing the meat with the back of a wooden spoon until it appears cooked but not browned. Add all the remaining ingredients except the parsley. Cook for another 7 to 8 minutes, stirring occasionally, until the liquid in the pan has evaporated and the mixture seems cohesive. Remove from the heat and stir in the parsley.

Place the eggplants, cut side up, in a foil-lined baking dish. Press down with a spoon to create a shallow well in each, and mound equal amounts of the turkey mixture into the wells. Bake for 15 minutes, then serve immediately.

*Yield—6 servings*
*Fat per serving—1.0 g.*

# Gnocchi with Tomato-Basil Sauce

These tiny Italian dumplings, presented here in a simple tomato sauce, are as light as the pillows they resemble.

GNOCCHI:

1 pound Yukon Gold potatoes
    (about 3 potatoes)
5 cups cold water
1 large egg, white only
³/₄ cup all-purpose flour

TOMATO-BASIL SAUCE:

One 28-ounce can peeled Italian-style
    plum tomatoes, with juice
½ cup chopped white onion
    (about 1 small onion)
1 clove garlic, finely chopped
1 tablespoon finely chopped fresh basil,
    plus additional for garnish
Dash of salt and freshly ground black
    pepper, to taste

To make the gnocchi, put the potatoes and water in a saucepan and cook for 30 minutes, uncovered, over medium heat. Drain and remove the potato skins while still hot by rubbing with a clean dish towel. Rice the peeled potatoes and let cool for 2 to 3 minutes. Add the egg white and flour and, with lightly floured hands, mix just until a cohesive soft dough is formed.

Break off small sections of dough and roll them out into 1-inch-thick ropes. Cut the ropes on the diagonal into ½-inch sections. Using a sharp pointed knife, make a partial incision in the middle of each gnocchi.

For the sauce, seed and finely chop the tomatoes, making sure to reserve the juice separately.

Combine the onion and 2 tablespoons of the juice from the tomatoes in a heavy saucepan. Cook over low heat for about 5 minutes, stirring occasionally, until the onion is soft. Add the garlic and cook for 2 minutes, stirring. Add the tomatoes and cook for 5 minutes, until the tomato starts to give off water. Add the basil, another 8 tablespoons of the reserved tomato juice, and a little salt and pepper, if desired. Simmer for 20 minutes, uncovered, until the sauce thickens.

Meanwhile, bring a large pot of water to a boil. Salt it lightly and lower the heat to a gentle simmer. Drop in 8 to 10 gnocchi at a time and cook for about 3 minutes. The gnocchi are done as soon as they rise to the top of the boiling water. Remove them with a slotted spoon and continue until all the gnocchi are done.

Serve about 12 gnocchi on each plate, topped with some tomato-basil sauce and a sprinkling of fresh basil.

*Yield — 4 servings*
*Fat per serving — 0.30 g.*

# Pasta Frittata

A great buffet item, this can be served warm or room temperature. It goes well with the crusty French Country Round (page 134).

5 sun-dried tomatoes (see Pantry)
1 clove garlic, minced
⅜ cup boiling water
1 cup nonfat liquid egg substitute
⅓ cup skim milk
¼ cup nonfat sour cream
½ tablespoon chopped fresh chives
1 tablespoon chopped fresh basil

1 cup cooked thin-strand pasta
  (see Pantry)
⅓ cup julienned zucchini
  (about 1 small zucchini)
⅓ cup seeded, julienned red bell pepper
½ tablespoon coarse kosher salt
¼ teaspoon freshly ground black pepper
Light vegetable oil spray

Preheat the oven to 300 degrees.

Combine the sun-dried tomatoes, garlic, and boiling water in a small bowl and set aside for about 10 minutes to reconstitute.

Whisk the egg substitute, milk, and sour cream together. Add the herbs and mix in the cooked pasta, zucchini, bell pepper, and seasonings. Drain the tomatoes, discarding the garlic. Slice the tomatoes thinly and add to the mixture.

Preheat a well-seasoned 9-inch cast-iron skillet. Spray once lightly with the vegetable oil spray and pour in the frittata batter. Place in the oven and bake for 20 to 25 minutes, until the edges are set and the frittata is slightly brown. Remove from the oven and cool for 10 to 15 minutes before slicing into 6 portions.

*Yield — 6 servings*
*Fat per serving — 0.34 g.*

# Fish and Vegetable Kebabs

8 ounces uncooked cod fillet, cut into
   1-inch chunks
2 tablespoons freshly squeezed lemon juice
¼ cup tarragon vinegar
⅓ cup trimmed and chopped scallions
   (3–4 scallions)
⅛ teaspoon white pepper
1 large red bell pepper (7–8 ounces),
   seeded and cut into 1-inch cubes

1 large green bell pepper, seeded and cut
   into 1-inch cubes
1 large white onion (about 8 ounces), cut
   into 1-inch cubes
Four 8-inch wooden skewers
2 cups cooked white rice

Combine the cod, lemon juice, vinegar, scallions, and white pepper in a nonreactive bowl, mixing to coat the fish well. Cover and marinate for 30 minutes in the refrigerator. Drain and pat the fish dry.

Preheat the broiler.

Thread an assortment of fish, peppers, and onion onto each skewer. (Placing the firm peppers at both ends will help hold the kebabs together.) Broil the kebabs for 6 minutes, turning once to brown evenly. Serve with the rice.

*Yield—4 servings*
*Fat per serving—0.71 g.*

A fat-free rendition of the classic kebab. It also pairs well with Saffron Rice or Wild Rice Risotto (page 125 or 130).

# Individual Chicken Potpies

### DOUGH:

1½ cups all-purpose flour
½ teaspoon salt
1 tablespoon chopped fresh dill
7 tablespoons plain nonfat yogurt
3 tablespoons buttermilk
1 tablespoon water

### FILLING:

6 sprigs fresh dill
4 ounces uncooked skinless, boneless
    chicken breast
2 carrots, peeled and thinly sliced on the
    diagonal (about 1 cup sliced carrots)
6 ounces whole white pearl onions,
    unpeeled

¾ cup canned or frozen corn kernels
¾ cup canned or frozen peas
2 tablespoons chopped fresh oregano
2 tablespoons chopped fresh rosemary
Dash of salt and freshly ground black
    pepper, to taste
2 cups 99% Fat-Free Chicken Stock
    (page 10)
2 tablespoons all-purpose flour

### GLAZE:

1 large egg, white only
½ tablespoon water

To make the dough, combine the flour, salt, and dill in a bowl and mix well with a fork. Add 4 tablespoons of the yogurt and mix to a sandy consistency. Repeat with the remaining yogurt. Add the buttermilk and water. Using a wooden spoon, blend just until a ball of dough is formed. Wrap the dough in plastic wrap, flatten it slightly into a patty, and refrigerate for 1 hour.

To make the filling, add the dill sprigs to water sufficient to fill the bottom of a steamer and bring to a boil over medium heat. Place the chicken in the steamer basket, cover, and steam for 15 minutes. Remove the chicken, replace with the carrots, re-cover, and steam for 5 minutes. Dice the steamed chicken into ¼-inch cubes.

Fill a small saucepan with water, bring to a boil, drop in the pearl onions, and cook for 3 minutes. Rinse the onions in cold water. Trim the root on each onion, then grasp the root end and gently squeeze toward the stem until the onion slips out of its skin.

Combine the corn kernels and peas in a small bowl.

Into each of four 10-ounce casseroles, put ⅜ cup corn-and-pea mixture, ¼ cup carrot, and about ⅛ cup pearl onions. Divide the cubed chicken among the 4 casseroles (about ⅛ cup each). Add ½ tablespoon oregano and ½ tablespoon rosemary to each. Dust with salt and freshly ground black pepper to taste, mix each casserole well, and set aside.

Roll out the dough on a lightly floured surface with a lightly floured rolling pin, to a 10-inch circle about ¼ inch thick. Form 4 small circles in the dough, using the top of a clean 10-ounce casserole as a guide, and cut them out with a knife.

Preheat the oven to 400 degrees.

Bring the chicken stock to a simmer in a saucepan over medium heat. While continuing to simmer, remove 2 tablespoons of the stock to a small bowl, add the flour, and stir until smooth. Add another 2 tablespoons of stock and stir to a thin paste. Remove the remaining stock from the heat and whisk in the paste until the mixture is smooth and free of lumps. Return to the heat and continue to simmer, stirring occasionally, just until thickened, about 5 minutes.

Place the casseroles on a baking sheet. Spoon ½ cup of the chicken stock mixture over each, and divide any remaining stock equally. Top each casserole with a dough round. Beat the egg white until frothy with the ½ tablespoon water and paint the dough with this mixture. Bake for 20 to 25 minutes, until golden and bubbly.

*Yield—4 servings*
*Fat per serving—1.0 g.*

# Shrimp Jambalaya

We think you will find this jambalaya every bit as good as the New Orleans version that inspired it—it has all of the taste with none of the fat.

1 cup chopped white onion (about
    1 medium onion)
⅓ cup seeded, chopped green bell pepper
⅓ cup seeded, chopped red bell pepper
1 tablespoon minced garlic (3–4 cloves)
1 cup seeded, chopped fresh tomato
    (about 1 large tomato)

½ teaspoon dried thyme
Up to ⅛ teaspoon cayenne pepper, to taste
2 cups 99% Fat-Free Chicken Stock
    (page 10)
1 cup uncooked long-grain white rice
4 ounces uncooked medium shrimp, peeled,
    deveined, and halved

Combine the onion, bell peppers, and garlic in a deep-sided non-stick frying pan. Cook for about 5 minutes over medium heat, stirring frequently, until the onion begins to turn golden. Stir in the tomato, thyme, and cayenne pepper. Add the stock, raise the heat to medium, and bring to a boil.

Add the rice and shrimp. Cover, reduce the heat to low, and simmer for 20 minutes. Serve hot.

Yield—4 servings
Fat per serving—0.78 g.

# Chinese Noodles with Shrimp and Chicken

1 ounce dried shiitake mushrooms
  (6–8 mushrooms)
1 cup boiling water
8 cups plus 3 tablespoons cold water
4 ounces nouilles batons (Chinese dried
  noodle sticks)
½ cup sliced white onion
1 teaspoon chopped garlic (1–1½ cloves)

1 teaspoon freshly grated ginger
3 ounces uncooked medium shrimp, peeled,
  deveined, and halved
3 ounces skinless smoked chicken breast,
  shredded
½ cup 99% Fat-Free Chicken Stock
  (page 10)
3 tablespoons soy sauce

In a small bowl, combine the dried mushrooms and boiling water. Set aside to soak for about 5 minutes.

In a pot, bring the 2 quarts cold water to a boil, add the noodles, and cook for 3 minutes. Drain the noodles in a colander and rinse under cold running water.

Remove the mushrooms from the soaking water, squeezing out any excess moisture. Stem and slice.

Combine the onion, garlic, and the 3 tablespoons cold water in a large, heavy frying pan. Cook for about 5 minutes over low heat, stirring often, until the onion turns limp. Add the ginger and shrimp and cook for about 2 minutes more, until the shrimp just begin to turn pink. Stir in the chicken, add the noodles, and toss. Stir in the chicken stock and soy sauce. Cook for an additional 30 seconds to 1 minute, until all the ingredients are incorporated. Serve immediately.

*Yield — 6 servings*
*Fat per serving — 0.88 g.*

Brimming with shiitake mushrooms, smoked chicken, and shrimp, redolent of fresh ginger—and tossed with delicate Chinese noodles—this is a stylish, light dinner that can be prepared in minutes.

# Almost Bill's Rice-and-Bean Special

This recipe is based upon one of our favorite dishes, developed by food columnist William Rice. To make it fat free, we removed the vegetable oil and replaced the ham with smoked turkey.

2 cups Spanish talosano beans or pinto beans, rinsed and picked over
2 small dried hot chile peppers
3 sprigs fresh thyme, plus ½ teaspoon minced fresh thyme
2 bay leaves
1 cup uncooked long-grain white rice
6 slices smoked bacon, cubed (see Pantry)
12 ounces uncooked skinless, boneless turkey breast
3 tablespoons water
1 cup chopped white onion (about 1 medium onion)

1 tablespoon minced garlic (about 3 cloves)
⅛ teaspoon ground allspice
⅛ teaspoon ground cinnamon
⅛ teaspoon ground nutmeg
1 cup cooked, coarsely chopped spinach
1 tablespoon wine vinegar, plus additional as condiment
Dash of freshly ground black pepper, to taste
Hot sauce, as condiment

Put the beans in a large saucepan and cover with water by 2 to 3 inches. Bring to a boil over medium heat. Remove from the heat. Drain and rinse the beans.

Return the beans to the pan and cover with 2 to 3 inches of fresh water. Add the dried chile peppers, the sprigs of thyme, and the bay leaves. Cover and simmer for 40 to 45 minutes.

About 20 minutes before the beans are done, cook the rice according to the package directions.

Fill the bottom of a steamer with water, add the bacon and bring to a boil. Make sure there is not enough water to boil up through the holes in the bottom of the steamer basket. If the turkey breast is whole, cut it into 3 to 4 pieces. When the water is boiling, place the turkey in the basket, cover, and steam for 15 minutes. Remove and chop.

Combine the 3 tablespoons water and the onion in a large skillet. Cook for about 5 minutes over medium heat, stirring, until the onion is soft. Add the garlic, minced thyme, and spices. Cook for 2 minutes more, stirring often. Add the chopped turkey and the spinach and heat through (about 5 minutes).

Stir the contents of the skillet into the cooked beans. Add the tablespoon of vinegar and a bit of pepper, if desired, and stir. If the mixture seems dry, add some water or stock.

Serve the beans over the cooked rice with hot sauce and vinegar on the side.

*Yield — 8 servings*
*Fat per serving — 0.94 g.*

# Scallops with Red Lentil Pilaf

The pale apricot of the cooked lentils contrasts strikingly with the pure white scallops, while the crunch of the lentils is juxtaposed against the smooth-textured shellfish.

*LENTIL PILAF:*
*2 tablespoons trimmed and chopped*
*    scallions (2–3 scallions)*
*⅓ cup seeded, diced green bell pepper*
*⅓ cup peeled, diced carrot (about 1 carrot)*
*½ cup peeled, diced zucchini (about 1*
*    small zucchini)*
*½ cup dried red lentils*
*1 cup 99% Fat-Free Chicken Stock*
*    (page 10)*

*½ teaspoon minced garlic*
*Dash of freshly ground black pepper,*
*    to taste*
*2 tablespoons chopped fresh parsley*

*SCALLOPS:*
*12 ounces uncooked bay scallops*
*½ cup dry white wine*
*Snipped fresh chives, for garnish*

To make the pilaf, combine the vegetables in a heavy frying pan. Cook for about 5 minutes over low heat, stirring constantly, until the scallion wilts.

Add the lentils, chicken stock, and garlic. Stir. Bring to a boil over medium heat, then lower the heat, cover, and simmer for 10 minutes. Stir in the black pepper and parsley. Take care not to overcook; the lentils should have a crunch.

While the lentils simmer, bring to a boil enough water to fill a shallow, flat-bottomed baking dish about halfway.

When the pilaf if done, transfer it to four 4-ounce custard cups. Place the cups in the baking dish to keep warm in the hot water while you cook the scallops.

Preheat a nonstick frying pan over medium heat. Add the scallops and cook for 30 seconds, stirring constantly. Add the wine and cook for another 2 minutes.

To serve, unmold each cup of pilaf in the center of a dinner plate. Encircle it with scallops and garnish with chives.

*Yield—4 servings*
*Fat per serving—0.92 g.*

# Pasta with Smoked Chicken and Pea Pods

9 ounces uncooked thin-strand pasta
  (see Pantry)
1 cup thinly sliced white onion (about
  1 medium onion)
1 tablespoon water
1 tablespoon coarsely chopped garlic
  (about 3 cloves)
4 ounces red bell pepper, seeded and thinly
  sliced

4 ounces Chinese pea pods
3 ounces skinless smoked chicken breast,
  thinly sliced
¼ cup shredded fresh basil
⅛ teaspoon salt
⅛ teaspoon freshly ground black pepper
1 cup 99% Fat-Free Chicken Stock
  (page 10)

Cook the pasta in a large pot of boiling water over high heat to desired tenderness (3 to 4 minutes for homemade or other fresh pasta, 8 to 10 minutes for dry). Drain and set aside.

Combine the onion and water in a nonstick frying pan. Cook for about 4 minutes over medium-low heat, shaking the pan a little, until the onion is wilted. Add the garlic, bell pepper, and pea pods. Cover and cook for 2 minutes. Add the chicken and seasonings, cover, and cook for another 5 minutes.

While this mixture is cooking, return the pasta to the pot and add the chicken stock. Cook over medium-low to medium heat, stirring, until most of the stock has been absorbed. Turn off the heat, add the chicken mixture, toss, and serve.

*Yield — 6 servings*
*Fat per serving — 0.83 g.*

A satisfying dish with Chinese overtones. Its rich, smoky flavor demonstrates how much can be achieved with the addition of just a little smoked poultry.

# Spicy Turkey Chili

This is a unique chili, set apart both by its firm, almost crunchy texture and by the inclusion of turkey meatballs.

12 ounces skinless turkey breast, ground (see Pantry)
2 tablespoons water
1 cup chopped white onion (about 1 medium onion)
¼ cup seeded, chopped green bell pepper
¼ cup seeded, chopped red bell pepper
½ tablespoon minced garlic (about 2 cloves)
One 28-ounce can peeled Italian-style plum tomatoes, with their juice

2 tablespoons white wine vinegar
2 tablespoons chopped fresh oregano
¼ cup chopped fresh cilantro, plus additional for garnish
1 teaspoon hot chili powder
1 teaspoon ground cumin
½ teaspoon cayenne pepper
⅛ teaspoon salt
1½ cups cooked white beans
6 tablespoons peeled, diced cucumber, for garnish

Roll the ground turkey into meatballs, using about 2 tablespoons for each meatball.

Put the meatballs into a heavy nonstick frying pan over medium-low heat. Shake the pan periodically to ensure that the meatballs cook evenly. Cook for about 5 minutes, just enough for the meatballs to brown lightly and form a slight crust, which will help them hold their shape. Transfer the meatballs to a heavy kettle or Dutch oven.

Combine the water, onion, bell peppers, and garlic in the frying pan. Cook for about 6 minutes over low heat, stirring frequently, until the onion is wilted and the pepper soft. Add the cooked vegetables to the turkey.

Add the tomatoes and their juice to the kettle, crushing the tomatoes slightly with the side of a spoon. Add all the remaining ingredients except the beans and cucumber; stir. Cover partially and simmer for 20 minutes over medium-low heat. Stir in the beans and simmer, uncovered, for 10 minutes more.

Garnish each serving with a little chopped cilantro and a tablespoon of diced cucumber.

*Yield — 6 servings*
*Fat per serving — 0.95 g.*

# Pasta in Garlic Sauce with Shrimp and Broccoli

10 cloves garlic
1 cup 99% Fat Free Chicken Stock
    (page 10)
7 ounces uncooked thin-strand pasta
    (see Pantry)
2 tablespoons water
1 pound broccoli flowerets (about
    1 large head)

½ cup sliced white onion (about
    1 small onion)
½ pound uncooked medium shrimp (about
    24), peeled, deveined, and halved
½ cup chopped fresh dill
⅛ teaspoon red pepper flakes
Dash of salt and freshly ground black
    pepper, to taste

This clear, thin garlic sauce is a noteworthy change from the heavy mound under which pasta typically is buried. It lends both a permeating flavor and a gloss to the pasta, set off by flecks of seafood and vegetables.

Put the garlic and stock in a small nonreactive saucepan and bring to a boil over medium heat. Reduce the heat to low and cover. Simmer for about 20 minutes, until the garlic is soft and easily mashed with a fork. Transfer the contents of the pan to a food processor or blender and puree until smooth. Set aside.

Bring a large pot of water to a boil. Add the pasta, stirring to make sure the strands don't stick together, and cook over high heat to desired tenderness (3 to 4 minutes for homemade or other fresh pasta, 8 to 10 minutes for dry).

Meanwhile, put 1 tablespoon of the water in a nonstick frying pan and bring to a boil over medium heat. Add the broccoli and onion, reduce the heat to low, cover, and cook for 3 minutes. Add the shrimp, dill, and the remaining tablespoon of water. Stir, recover, and cook for 4 to 5 minutes more, until the shrimp turn pink. Remove from the heat.

When the pasta is done, drain it in a colander and return it to the pot over very low heat. Add the garlic puree and mix well to coat the pasta. Add the broccoli-shrimp mixture and the seasonings. Toss together until well blended and serve immediately.

*Yield—6 servings*
*Fat per serving—1.0 g.*

# Cumin Noodles

This dish combines culinary influences from the American Southwest and the Pacific rim to create an interesting medley of flavors.

2 tablespoons soy sauce
6 ounces uncooked skinless, boneless chicken breast, thinly sliced
12 ounces soba noodles (Japanese buckwheat noodles)
2 tablespoons water
4 ounces snow peas, trimmed and quartered

1 teaspoon chopped garlic (1–1½ cloves)
¾ cup 99% Fat-Free Chicken Stock (page 10)
1½ teaspoons ground cumin
2 tablespoons chopped fresh cilantro
3 scallions (about 3 ounces total), trimmed and julienned
½ teaspoon freshly ground black pepper

Fill a large saucepan with water and bring to a boil.

Meanwhile, combine ½ tablespoon of the soy sauce with the sliced chicken and mix to coat the chicken well. Set aside.

When the water boils, add the noodles and cook for 2 minutes over high heat. Drain and rinse under cold running water.

Put the 2 tablespoons of water into a deep-sided nonstick frying pan over low heat. When warm, add the chicken and the snow peas and cook for 3 minutes, stirring constantly. Add the garlic and cook for 1 minute more.

Raise the heat to medium. Add the drained noodles, the chicken stock, the remaining 1½ tablespoons soy sauce, and the cumin. Toss. Add the cilantro, scallions, and pepper. Cook for another 2 minutes, again stirring constantly. Serve immediately.

*Yield — 6 servings*
*Fat per serving — 0.97 g.*

# Chicken Vesuvio

6 ounces uncooked skinless, boneless
  chicken breast
2 medium red potatoes (about 5 ounces
  each), cut into 8 spears each
¼ pound white button mushrooms,
  stemmed and cut into large chunks
One 14-ounce can artichoke bottoms,
  drained and halved

2 tablespoons freshly squeezed lemon juice
2 tablespoons pear nectar
½ tablespoon chopped garlic (about
  2 cloves)
½ tablespoon chopped fresh rosemary

Trim any excess fat from the chicken breast and cut the breast into 2-inch cubes.

Combine the chicken cubes, potato spears, mushrooms, and artichokes in a very large bowl.

Mix the remaining ingredients thoroughly and pour on top. Toss to coat well. Cover and marinate in the refrigerator for at least 30 minutes.

Preheat the oven to 450 degrees.

Transfer the mixture to a baking dish large enough to hold all the ingredients in a single layer. Bake for 20 minutes.

Yield—4 servings
Fat per serving—0.93 g.

We replaced oil with pear nectar for this old Chicago favorite, which is a garlic lover's delight. Our version comes out crisp and imbued with a subtle hue from the nectar.

# Chicken Tacos with Jicama Salsa

We serve these tacos soft, in the traditional Mexican manner, rather than frying the tortillas before stuffing them. The cool salsa, thick and filled with jicama chunks, provides a nice contrast in temperature and texture.

*Eight 7-inch corn tortillas*

*FILLING:*
*6 slices smoked bacon, cut into cubes (see Pantry)*
*6 ounces uncooked skinless, boneless chicken breast*
*1½ tablespoons chopped fresh cilantro*
*2 tablespoons water*
*½ teaspoon seeded, finely chopped fresh jalapeño pepper*
*1 cup chopped spinach (chop spinach in strips crosswise)*

*JICAMA SALSA:*
*1 cup seeded, chopped yellow tomato (about 1 tomato)*
*1 cup peeled, finely diced jicama*
*¼ cup coarsely chopped red onion*
*2 tablespoons seeded, coarsely chopped fresh jalapeño pepper (about 1 small jalapeño)*
*½ tablespoon finely chopped garlic (about 2 cloves)*
*2 teaspoons freshly squeezed lime juice*
*2 tablespoons chopped fresh cilantro*

Preheat the oven to its lowest setting.

Wrap the tortillas in a clean kitchen towel and place them in the oven to keep warm.

Fill the bottom of a steamer with water and add the bacon. Bring to a boil, making sure there is not enough water to boil up through the holes in the bottom of the steamer basket. If the chicken breast is whole, cut it into 3 or 4 pieces. When the water is boiling, place the chicken in the basket, cover, and steam for 15 minutes. Remove and shred the chicken.

To make the salsa, mix the tomato, jicama, and onion well. Mix in the remaining salsa ingredients and set aside.

Place 4 dinner plates in the oven to warm.

To make the filling, combine the shredded chicken, water, cilantro, and jalapeño pepper in a small nonstick frying pan over medium heat. Cook for 1 to 2 minutes, stirring constantly, just to heat through (be careful not to dry out the chicken).

Remove the tortillas and dinner plates from the oven. Assemble the tacos by spreading a little spinach in the center of each and topping it with the chicken mixture. Roll each one into a cylinder and place 2 tacos on each warmed dinner plate. Surround with the salsa and serve immediately.

*Yield — 4 servings*
*Fat per serving — 0.86 g.*

# Curried Lobster Risotto

This dish is made for entertaining. Everyone loves lobster. We keep lobster tails on hand in the freezer so that we can put this together on barely a moment's notice. The preparation time for a thick, creamy risotto is brief. You can even put your guests to work stirring the rice.

*5 cups 99% Fat-Free Chicken Stock (page 10)*
*4 ounces snow peas, trimmed and cut into quarters on the diagonal*
*Six 3-ounce uncooked warm-water lobster tails (such as rock lobster)*
*⅓ cup chopped shallots (about 2 large shallots)*
*½ tablespoon minced garlic (about 2 cloves)*
*2 tablespoons water*
*1½ cups uncooked arborio rice*
*½ cup chopped fresh parsley, loosely packed*
*½ tablespoon curry powder*

Bring the chicken stock to a boil, lower the heat, and maintain at a simmer.

Fill a small saucepan about three quarters full with water and bring to a boil over high heat. Add the snow peas and blanch for 20 seconds. Immediately drain and rinse under cold water. Set aside.

Fill the bottom of a steamer with water and bring to a boil. Add the lobster, cover, and steam for about 5 minutes, until the shells turn red. Cool a bit, then cut the soft white underside with scissors, remove the meat, and slice it into medallions.

Combine the shallots, garlic, and water in a heavy-bottomed saucepan. Cook for 4 minutes over low heat, stirring constantly. Add the rice and cook, stirring, for another 3 minutes.

Slowly add ½ cup of the hot stock, stirring constantly. Allow to come to a simmer. Once the stock has been absorbed, add another ½ cup of stock and bring back to a simmer, always stirring.

Continue adding hot stock, ½ cup at a time. When only about 1 cup of stock remains to be added, stir the snow peas, lobster, parsley, and curry powder into the rice, then add ½ cup of chicken stock and stir until absorbed. Add the remaining ½ cup of stock and stir until all the stock is absorbed and the rice is creamy. Preparation of this risotto should take 15 to 20 minutes from the first addition of stock. Serve immediately.

*Yield — 6 servings*
*Fat per serving — 0.97 g.*

# Shrimp and Leek Risotto

The quality of the rice is critical to any risotto; it's best made from arborio. We seal the kernels by adding them to the hot pan in which the vegetables have been prepared, rather than coating them with butter. The whole dish can be made in less than half an hour, but vigilance and careful attention to stirring the rice are crucial.

6 cups 99% Fat-Free Chicken Stock (page 10)
1 cup trimmed, sliced leek, white and light green parts only (about 4 ounces trimmed)
2 cups uncooked arborio rice
1 cup dry white wine
½ pound uncooked medium shrimp, peeled, deveined, and cut into chunks
Dash of salt and freshly ground black pepper, to taste
4 teaspoons freshly grated Parmesan cheese

Bring the stock to a boil over medium heat. Lower the heat and keep at a constant simmer.

Put the leek in a heavy saucepan and sauté dry over low heat for about 5 minutes, stirring constantly, until soft. Add the rice and cook, stirring constantly, for 2 minutes.

Slowly add 1½ cups of the hot stock, stirring constantly. Allow the liquid to come to a simmer. Once the stock has been absorbed, add another 1½ cups and bring the mixture back to a simmer, stirring constantly. When this additional stock has been absorbed, stir in the wine and shrimp.

Continue adding hot stock, ½ cup at a time, until absorbed, stirring constantly, until the risotto is tender and creamy. The entire process, from addition of the first 1½ cups of stock, should take 20 to 25 minutes.

Stir in a dash of salt and pepper, along with the grated cheese. Serve immediately.

Yield—8 servings
Fat per serving—0.79 g.

# 6

## *Side*

# DISHES

# Gratin of Root Vegetables

9 ounces rutabaga, peeled
12 ounces sweet potato, peeled
6 ounces parsnip, peeled
2 ounces parsley root, peeled
1 teaspoon ground nutmeg

Dash of salt and freshly ground black
  pepper, to taste
9 ounces leek, trimmed and thinly sliced
1 cup buttermilk

Preheat the oven to 400 degrees.

Very thinly slice the rutabaga, sweet potato, parsnip, and parsley root with a mandoline cutter.

Layer the rutabaga slices on the bottom of a gratin dish. Sprinkle about ¼ teaspoon of the nutmeg on top and lightly dust with salt and pepper. Top with layers of sweet potato and parsnip, sprinkling ¼ teaspoon of nutmeg and a dash of salt and pepper between each layer. Layer the leek on top, leaving an open circle in the center. Place the parsley root in the circle. Dust the top with salt, pepper, and the remaining nutmeg. Carefully pour the buttermilk down the sides and into the center of the dish.

Bake for 30 to 35 minutes, until the top has browned.

*Yield—8 servings*
*Fat per serving—0.69 g.*

This is the most complex of our gratins. The flavors of the root vegetables, sliced paper thin and layered, intermingle with the creamy buttermilk and the hint of sweetness provided by the nutmeg.

# Steamed Bitter Greens

This is basic and satisfying fare that goes well with such poultry dishes as Turkey Medallions (page 84).

*4 ounces turnip greens, trimmed*
*4 ounces mustard greens, trimmed*
*4 ounces spinach, trimmed*

*4 strips smoked bacon, cut into cubes*
  *(see Pantry)*
*1 teaspoon rice wine vinegar*

Tear the mustard greens and spinach leaves in half, the turnip greens in thirds. Rinse thoroughly under cold running water, taking care to pick out any residual grit. Set aside to drain.

Fill the bottom of a steamer with water and add the bacon. Bring to a boil, taking care that the water level is not high enough to boil up through the holes in the bottom of the steamer basket. Put the greens in the steamer basket, cover, and steam for about 3 minutes, until wilted.

Toss in the vinegar before serving.

*Yield—4 servings*
*Fat per serving—0.18 g.*

# Couscous with Vegetables

1½ cups 99% Fat-Free Chicken Stock
    (page 10)
1 cup uncooked couscous
One 8-ounce can garbanzo beans, rinsed
    and drained
1 teaspoon chopped garlic (about 1 clove)
½ cup finely chopped yellow onion
⅔ cup seeded, roughly chopped yellow
    bell pepper
½ cup trimmed and chopped celery
    (about 1 stalk)

½ cup peeled, finely chopped carrot
    (about 1 small carrot)
¼ cup water
2 tablespoons sherry
¼ teaspoon freshly ground black pepper
¼ teaspoon ground allspice
⅛ teaspoon ground mace
½ teaspoon salt

Bring the stock to boil in a saucepan. Stir in the couscous, cover, and remove from the heat. After 5 minutes, fluff the couscous, re-cover, and set aside.

Combine the garbanzo beans, garlic, vegetables, water, and sherry in a nonstick frying pan. Cover and cook for 10 minutes over medium heat. Add the seasonings and stir.

To serve, ring the couscous around a platter and mound the vegetable mixture in the center.

*Yield—6 servings*
*Fat per serving—0.43 g.*

# Stuffed Zucchini

One 4-ounce red bell pepper
4 baby zucchini (about 1 pound total),
    trimmed
¼ cup plus 2 tablespoons water
¼ cup chopped white onion
1 teaspoon finely chopped garlic
    (about 1 clove)
½ cup seeded, finely chopped tomato
Dash of freshly ground black pepper,
    to taste

1 teaspoon dried fines herbes (a French
    seasoning mixture, available in most
    supermarkets)
½ teaspoon coarse kosher salt
⅓ cup cooked pearled barley
½ teaspoon freshly grated Parmesan
    cheese

Preheat the broiler and line the rack with aluminum foil.

Cut the bell pepper in half lengthwise, core, and seed.

Place the pepper on the rack, cut side down, 2 to 3 inches from the heat source. Broil for about 5 minutes, until charred. Remove the pepper carefully, leaving the broiler on.

Seal the pepper in an airtight plastic bag and let cool for about 10 minutes. Remove from the plastic bag, rub off the skin, and chop. (This should yield about ¼ cup chopped pepper.)

Cut a thin slice off the entire top length of each zucchini, and a partial slice in the center of the bottom side, just enough to allow the zucchini to set flat. Hollow out the zucchini by making a rectangular incision around the top, leaving a ¼-inch outer border. Scoop out, chop, and reserve the meat.

Place the zucchini, hollowed side down, in a small nonstick frying pan. Add the ¼ cup water and cook for 5 minutes over medium heat.

Meanwhile, combine the chopped zucchini, onion, garlic, tomato, black pepper to taste, chopped roasted bell pepper, and the 2 tablespoons water in another small pan. Cook, uncovered, for about 7 minutes over medium-low heat, until all the liquid in the pan (including that given off by the vegetables) has evaporated.

Transfer the mixture to a bowl and add the fine herbes, salt, and barley. Mix well and spoon into the hollow cavities of the zucchini. Sprinkle with the Parmesan cheese. Place on a foil-lined shallow baking dish and broil for about 2 minutes, until the tops of the stuffed zucchini are browned and crusty.

*Yield—4 servings*
*Fat per serving—0.51 g.*

# Horseradish Mashed Potatoes

Celery root and parsley root add character to this unusual variation on the once basic mashed potato. The addition of horseradish gives the combination a special zest.

4 ounces celery root, peeled and cut into chunks
8 ounces red potatoes (about 2 medium potatoes), peeled and cut into chunks
¼ cup peeled, chopped parsley root

½ teaspoon chopped garlic
1 teaspoon prepared white horseradish
⅛ teaspoon white pepper
¼ teaspoon coarse kosher salt
¼ cup buttermilk

Bring a saucepan of water to a boil over high heat. Add the celery root and cook for 5 minutes, uncovered. Add the potatoes and parsley root. Cook for another 15 minutes, then drain.

Put the mixture through a ricer into a serving bowl. Add the remaining ingredients, stir with a fork, and serve.

*Yield — 4 servings*
*Fat per serving — 0.29 g.*

# Cajun Red Beans and Rice

1 cup chopped white onion
   (about 1 medium onion)
¼ cup trimmed, chopped scallions
   (2–3 scallions)
½ tablespoon minced garlic
   (about 2 cloves)
⅔ cup seeded, chopped yellow bell pepper
Two 15-ounce cans red kidney beans,
   drained and rinsed

3½ ounces skinless smoked turkey breast,
   chopped
2 cups 99% Fat-Free Smoked Turkey
   Stock (page 8)
2 cups cooked white rice
¼ teaspoon freshly ground black pepper
½ teaspoon dried thyme
1 bay leaf
½ teaspoon salt

Combine the onion, scallions, garlic, and bell pepper in a saucepan. Cook for about 5 minutes over medium-low heat, until the onion turns translucent.

Add all the remaining ingredients. Bring to a boil over medium heat, cover, reduce the heat, and simmer for 30 minutes.

*Yield—6 servings (4 servings as main course)*
*Fat per serving—0.64 g. (0.96 g. as main course)*

# Turnip Gratin

1 tablespoon chopped garlic (3–4 cloves)
1 pound turnips (3–4 turnips), peeled and
    cut into ⅛-inch slices
2 teaspoons dried fines herbes (a French
    seasoning mixture, available in most
    supermarkets)
Dash of salt and freshly ground black
    pepper, to taste

½ pound red potatoes (about 2 small
    potatoes), peeled and sliced ⅛ inch thick
½ cup buttermilk
½ cup homemade bread crumbs
    (see Pantry)

Preheat the oven to 400 degrees.

Sprinkle 1 teaspoon of the garlic on the bottom of a gratin dish. Layer with about half the turnip slices. Sprinkle with half the fines herbes and a dash of salt and pepper.

Scatter a second teaspoon of garlic over the seasoned turnip slices, then add a layer of potato slices. Top with the remaining fines herbes, another dusting of salt and pepper, and the rest of the garlic.

Arrange the final layer of turnip slices on top, pour the buttermilk over all, and top with the bread crumbs.

Bake for 35 to 40 minutes, until the bread crumbs are brown.

*Yield — 6 servings*
*Fat per serving — 0.31 g.*

# Smoked Okra

4 slices smoked bacon, cut into cubes (see Pantry)

1 pound small okra pods, trimmed
¼ cup rice wine vinegar

Fill the bottom of a steamer with water, add the bacon, and bring to a boil, making sure there is not enough water to boil up through the holes in the bottom of the steamer basket. Put the okra into the basket, cover, and steam for 3 to 4 minutes, until fork tender.

Turn immediately into a warm serving dish, toss with the vinegar, and serve.

*Yield—4 servings*
*Fat per serving—0.10 g.*

Everything old is new again. Long in culinary limbo, okra has been rediscovered by a new generation of home cooks. This pleasantly smoky update eschews the fats of traditional Southern cooking and renders the pods drier and crisper. A great alternative to string beans.

# Turnip and Onion Puree

10 ounces turnip, peeled and cut into
 eighths (about 1 large turnip)
10 ounces white onion, quartered
 (about 1 medium onion)
2 ounces new red potato, peeled and halved
 (about 1 small potato)

⅛ teaspoon ground nutmeg
⅛ teaspoon freshly ground black pepper
¼ cup buttermilk

Combine the turnip, onion, and potato in a saucepan and add water to cover. Bring to a boil over medium heat, cover, and cook for about 20 minutes, until the vegetables are fork tender.

Drain and transfer the vegetables to a food processor or blender. Add the nutmeg and pepper. Puree to a smooth consistency, while gradually adding the buttermilk.

Return the puree to the saucepan and bring to a boil over medium heat. Stir and serve immediately.

*Yield—4 servings*
*Fat per serving—0.36 g.*

# Cumin Rice with Black Beans

½ cup peeled, chopped carrot (about
   1 small carrot)
½ cup chopped white onion
1 teaspoon chopped garlic (about 1 clove)
½ teaspoon chopped fresh thyme
1 teaspoon ground cumin
¼ teaspoon dried coriander

½ teaspoon salt
1 cup uncooked long-grain white rice
1 cup cooked black beans
1²⁄₃ cups 99% Fat-Free Chicken Stock
   (page 10)
2 tablespoons chopped fresh cilantro
1 tablespoon freshly squeezed lime juice

Combine the carrot, onion, and garlic in a saucepan and cook for 5 minutes over low heat, until the onion is wilted, stirring constantly. Add the thyme, cumin, coriander, and salt, then stir in the rice. Add the beans and stock, raise the heat to medium-high, and bring to a boil. Cover, lower the heat, and simmer for 15 minutes.

   Stir in the cilantro and lime juice and serve.

*Yield—4 servings*
*Fat per serving—0.44 g.*

We made this dish, which was inspired by Cuban black beans and rice, healthier and thicker in texture, adding some new seasoning twists in the process.

# Corn and Carrot Puree

1 cup peeled, chunked carrots (about 2 carrots)
½ cup corn kernels (about 1 small ear)
½ cup water

¼ cup buttermilk
⅛ teaspoon freshly ground black pepper
⅛ teaspoon ground nutmeg
Snipped fresh chives, for garnish

Combine the carrots, corn, and water in a small, heavy-bottomed saucepan. Bring to a boil over medium heat, taking care not to boil off the water. Cover, reduce the heat, and simmer for about 10 minutes, until the carrots are fork tender.

Drain and transfer the solid ingredients to a food processor or blender and puree to a smooth consistency. Return the puree to the pan, and whisk in the buttermilk, pepper, and nutmeg. Warm for about 1 minute over low heat. Sprinkle with the chives and serve.

*Yield—4 servings*
*Fat per serving—0.45 g.*

# Oven-Baked Potato Chips

2 medium red potatoes (about 10 ounces total)

Light vegetable oil cooking spray
1 teaspoon celery salt

Preheat the oven to 350 degrees.

Slice the potatoes very thin, using a mandoline slicer.

Lightly spray a nonstick baking sheet twice with the vegetable oil spray and distribute the oil evenly over the surface.

Arrange the potato slices in a single layer on the baking sheet. Bake for 5 minutes, then turn the slices over. After another 5 minutes, sprinkle with about half the celery salt, flip again, and sprinkle the other side with the remaining salt. Bake for 5 minutes more, until crisp and browned.

*Yield—4 servings*
*Fat per serving—0.65 g. (about 15 chips)*

Simple, healthful, and quite satisfying, oven-baked potatoes can stand alone as a light snack or accompany a salad, sandwiches, or soup. Heap them in a colorfully lined, decorative wicker basket.

# Minted Pea Puree

¼ cup chopped fresh mint
1 cup shelled peas (about 1 pound pods)
¾ cup water

1 tablespoon skim milk
⅛ teaspoon freshly ground black pepper

Put the mint, peas, and water in a small saucepan and bring to a boil over medium heat. Simmer for 10 to 15 minutes, uncovered, until the peas are easily mashed with a fork.

Drain and transfer the solid ingredients to the bowl of a food processor or blender and puree until smooth.

Return the mixture to the saucepan over low heat. Whisk in the milk and pepper and heat through, about 1 minute. Serve immediately.

*Yield — 4 servings*
*Fat per serving — 0.28 g.*

# Saffron Rice

½ cup diced yellow onion (about
  1 small onion)
½ cup seeded, diced red bell pepper
1 teaspoon finely chopped garlic
  (about 1 clove)
2 tablespoons water
1 cup uncooked long-grain white rice
½ cup shelled peas (about 8 ounces pods)

Scant ⅛ teaspoon saffron threads
1¼ cups 99% Fat-Free Chicken Stock
  (page 10)
¼ teaspoon salt
⅛ teaspoon freshly ground black pepper
¼ teaspoon dried thyme
¼ teaspoon dried oregano
Chopped fresh parsley, for garnish

Combine the onion, bell pepper, garlic, and water in a saucepan.
Cook for 4 minutes over medium-low heat, stirring occasionally.
Add the rice, peas, and saffron. Cook for 30 seconds, stirring constantly. Stir in the stock and seasonings. Raise the heat to medium and bring to a boil. Cover, lower the heat, and simmer for 15 minutes.

Garnish with parsley before serving.

*Yield—4 servings*
*Fat per serving—0.16 g.*

This vibrant yellow rice, which derives its distinctive color from the saffron, will be instantly recognizable to devotees of Spanish cuisine as the basis for paella.

We think risotto is just about perfect for any occasion—it can serve as hearty and homey comfort food or stylish party fare equally well. It's extraordinarily simple once you get the hang of the stirring, and it can be made in a matter of minutes.

# Risotto with Asparagus Tips and Shiitake Mushrooms

4 large dried shiitake mushrooms (about
  ¾ ounce)
2 cups hot water
1½ cups trimmed asparagus tips (about 8
  ounces)
2½ cups 99% Fat-Free Chicken Stock
  (page 10)

1 cup uncooked arborio rice
½ cup dry white wine
Dash of salt and freshly ground black
  pepper, to taste
1 tablespoon chopped flat-leaf parsley
3 teaspoons freshly grated Parmesan
  cheese

Place the mushrooms in the hot water and soak for 15 minutes.

Microwave the asparagus tips for 1 minute at full power and set aside.

Put the chicken stock in a small saucepan and bring to a boil over medium heat. Lower the heat and maintain at a simmer.

Remove the mushrooms from their soaking liquid. Strain 1 cup of the liquid into a measuring cup and reserve it. Cut away the woody stems of the mushrooms and slice them into matchsticks.

Put the rice in a heavy saucepan and warm it over low heat, stirring constantly, for 1 minute. While continuing to stir, slowly add 1 cup of the hot stock. Bring to a simmer, and, when the stock has been absorbed into the rice, stir in the reserved cup of strained mushroom water and bring back to a simmer. When this liquid has been absorbed, stir in the mushrooms, asparagus, and wine.

Continue to add stock, ½ cup at a time, stirring constantly, until the rice is creamy and tender. The total cooking time from addition of the first cup of stock is 15 to 20 minutes.

Stir in the salt and pepper, if desired, and the parsley. Sprinkle ½ teaspoon of Parmesan cheese over each portion and serve immediately.

*Yield — 6 servings*
*Fat per serving — 0.40 g.*

# Mushroom Basmati

We've limited the ingredients in this dish to showcase the hearty, aromatic personality of the domestic brown rice.

½ cup trimmed and chopped celery (about 1 stalk)
½ cup chopped yellow onion (about 1 small onion)
1 teaspoon chopped garlic (about 1 clove)
1 teaspoon chopped fresh thyme
¼ teaspoon ground sage
1 cup sliced white button mushrooms (about 4 ounces)

½ teaspoon salt
⅛ teaspoon freshly ground black pepper
1 cup uncooked domestic basmati brown rice
2 cups 99% Fat-Free Chicken Stock (page 10)

Combine the celery, onion, and garlic in a saucepan and cook for 5 minutes over low heat, stirring constantly. Stir in the thyme and sage. Add the mushrooms and stir. Stir in the salt and pepper. Add the rice, mix for 30 seconds, then add the stock. Raise the heat and bring to a boil. Stir, cover, lower the heat, and simmer for 45 minutes.

Remove from the heat and set aside, covered, for 5 minutes more before serving.

*Yield — 4 servings*
*Fat per serving — 0.16 g.*

# Potato and Squash Gratin

10 ounces red potatoes (about 2 potatoes), peeled
1 pound acorn squash (about 1 medium squash), peeled and seeded
1 pound butternut squash (about ½ medium squash), peeled and seeded

Dash of salt and freshly ground black pepper, to taste
½ cup buttermilk

Preheat the oven to 350 degrees.

Slice the potatoes and squash very thin using a mandoline slicer.

Layer about half the potato slices on the bottom of a gratin dish. Lightly dust with salt and pepper. Top with layers of butternut squash, acorn squash, and a final layer of potato, lightly dusting each layer with salt and pepper to taste. Pour the buttermilk over and around the contents of the dish.

Bake for 30 to 35 minutes, until the top has browned.

*Yield — 6 servings*
*Fat per serving — 0.32 g.*

# Wild Rice Risotto

The nutty crunchiness of the wild rice contrasts with the smooth, creamy arborio.

5 cups 99% Fat-Free Chicken Stock
  (page 10)
⅓ cup chopped shallots (about 2
  large shallots)
½ tablespoon minced garlic
  (about 2 cloves)

2 tablespoons water
½ cup uncooked wild rice
1 cup uncooked arborio rice
½ cup seeded, diced red bell pepper
¾ cup corn kernels (about 1 ear)
⅓ cup chopped flat-leaf parsley

Bring the chicken stock to a boil, lower the heat, and maintain at a simmer.

Combine the shallots, garlic, and water in a heavy-bottomed saucepan. Cook for 4 minutes over low heat, stirring constantly. Add the wild rice, stir, and cook for 15 seconds. Add ¾ cup of the chicken stock, cover, and simmer for 15 minutes.

Add the arborio rice and slowly stir in another ¾ cup of the stock. Bring to a simmer. When the stock has been completely absorbed, add another ½ cup, stirring constantly, and bring back to a simmer.

Continue adding hot stock, ½ cup at a time. With the last addition, stir in the bell pepper and corn. Cook, stirring constantly, until all the stock is absorbed and the rice is creamy. The preparation should take 15 to 20 minutes from the addition of the arborio rice. Stir in the parsley and serve immediately.

Yield—8 servings
Fat per serving—0.36 g.

7

# BREADS

# Hearty Stout Bread

¼ cup buttermilk
¼ cup sugar
2 cups all-purpose flour
1 cup stone-ground rye flour
½ teaspoon baking soda

1 teaspoon baking powder
½ teaspoon salt
½ teaspoon caraway seeds
12 ounces dark, heavy-bodied stout
Light vegetable oil cooking spray

Preheat the oven to 350 degrees.

Put the buttermilk in a small bowl and whisk in the sugar until dissolved. Set aside.

Combine the dry ingredients in a large mixing bowl and form a well in the center. Pour in the buttermilk mixture and the stout. Stir with a wooden spoon just until blended.

Spray a 9¼-inch loaf pan once lightly with vegetable oil spray and distribute the oil evenly over the surface of the pan. Pour in the batter. Bake for 40 to 45 minutes, until the loaf begins to separate from the edges of the pan and a tester inserted into the center comes out clean.

*Yield — 16 slices*
*Fat per slice — 0.35 g.*

A dense, coarse bread that goes well with soups, stews, and chilies.

# French Country Round

This crusty bread is extremely versatile. We serve it whole for dinner, slice it for sandwiches, and use it for croutons and bread crumbs.

1½ cups skim milk
2½ teaspoons active dry yeast (1 packet)
2 teaspoons salt
1 teaspoon sugar
3 cups all-purpose flour, plus a little
   extra for flouring during preparation

1 tablespoon cornmeal (if using a
   baking sheet)
4 ice cubes

Put the milk in a saucepan and scald over medium heat just until bubbly around the edges, making sure not to bring to a full boil. Remove from the heat and cool for a few minutes to lukewarm (105 to 115 degrees on an instant-read thermometer).

Combine ¾ cup of the lukewarm milk and the yeast in a small bowl and set aside for about 10 minutes to proof. (The mixture will begin to bubble.)

Combine the salt and sugar in a large mixing bowl. Mix in the proofed yeast and the remaining ¾ cup of milk. Continue to mix until well combined. Using a wooden spoon, gently mix in the flour, 1 cup at a time, until completely incorporated.

Transfer the dough to a lightly floured surface and gently knead for about 8 minutes, until it is smooth and elastic, and springs back to the touch. Form into a ball, flour lightly, and place in a warm, ungreased bowl. Cover with a damp cloth and set aside until the dough has doubled in size. (This should take about 2 hours in a warm kitchen.)

Punch the dough down to flatten it and remove it from the bowl. Form into a round loaf and place on a baking sheet sprinkled with cornmeal or on a baking stone. Cover and allow the dough to double a second time, about 1 hour.

Preheat the oven to 400 degrees.

Cut an "X" on the top of the loaf with a sharp knife. Place the baking sheet or baking stone on the middle rack and ice cubes on the bottom of the oven to create vapor. Bake for 30 to 40 minutes, until lightly brown. The loaf is done if it sounds hollow when lightly tapped on the bottom.

*Yield — 12 slices*
*Fat per slice — 0.31 g.*

# Herbed Sandwich Braid

1½ cups lukewarm water (105 to 115 degrees on an instant-read thermometer)

2½ teaspoons active dry yeast (1 packet)

½ teaspoon salt

½ tablespoon chopped fresh dill

1 teaspoon sugar

3 cups bread flour, plus a little extra for flouring during preparation

1 tablespoon cornmeal (if using a baking sheet)

2 ice cubes

Combine ¾ cup of the lukewarm water and the yeast in a small bowl and set aside for about 10 minutes to proof. (The mixture will begin to bubble.)

Combine the salt, dill, and sugar in a large mixing bowl. Mix in the proofed yeast and the remaining ¾ cup of water. Mix well. Using a wooden spoon, gently mix in the flour, 1 cup at a time, until completely incorporated.

Transfer the dough to a lightly floured surface and knead gently for about 8 minutes, until the dough is smooth and elastic, and springs back to the touch. Form into a ball, flour lightly, and place in a warm, ungreased bowl. Cover with a damp cloth and set aside for about 2 hours in a warm place, until the dough has doubled in size.

Punch the dough down to flatten it and remove it from the bowl. Divide the dough into 3 equal portions. Flour your hands lightly and work each portion into a long thin rope about 1 inch in diameter.

Lay the strips side by side about ½ inch apart on a lightly floured surface. Crimp them together at one end and braid the strips, tucking the ends under. Carefully transfer the braided loaf to a baking sheet sprinkled with cornmeal or to a baking stone. Cover and set aside for about 1 hour, until doubled in size.

Preheat the oven to 400 degrees.

Place the baking sheet or baking stone on the middle rack and the ice cubes on the bottom of the oven to create vapor. Bake for 30 to 40 minutes, until lightly browned. The loaf is done if it sounds hollow when lightly tapped on the bottom.

*Yield — 24 slices*
*Fat per slice — 0.26 g.*

# Earl Grey Dinner Rolls

The Earl Grey tea imparts a rich, browned appearance usually achieved by painting rolls with egg yolk. It also lends a flavor redolent of cardamom.

1½ cups boiling water
2 Earl Grey tea bags
2½ teaspoons active dry yeast
    (1 packet)
2 teaspoons salt
1 teaspoon sugar

3 cups all-purpose flour, plus a little extra
    for flouring during preparation
1 tablespoon cornmeal
3 ice cubes

Combine the boiling water and tea bags in a bowl and set aside to steep for a few minutes, until tea cools to lukewarm (105 to 115 degrees on an instant-read thermometer).

Remove ¾ cup of the lukewarm tea to a small bowl. Add the yeast and set aside for about 10 minutes to proof. (The mixture will begin to bubble.)

Combine the salt and sugar in a large mixing bowl. Mix in the proofed yeast and the remaining ¾ cup of tea. Continue to mix until well combined. Using a wooden spoon, gently mix in the flour, 1 cup at a time, until completely incorporated.

Transfer the dough to a lightly floured surface and knead gently for about 8 minutes, until the dough is smooth and elastic, and springs back to the touch. Form it into a ball, flour lightly, and place in a warm, ungreased bowl. Cover with a damp cloth and set aside for about 2 hours, until the dough has doubled in size.

Punch the dough down to flatten it and remove it from the bowl. Cut the dough into 12 equal pieces, shape each piece into an oval, and place the ovals on a heavy cookie sheet sprinkled with cornmeal. Cover, and allow the dough to double a second time, about 1 hour.

Preheat the oven to 400 degrees.

Cut a slit down the center on the top of each oval with a sharp knife. Place the baking sheet on the middle rack of the oven and the ice cubes on the bottom to create vapor. Bake the rolls for 20 to 25 minutes, until lightly browned. The rolls are done if they sound hollow when lightly tapped on the bottom.

*Yield—12 rolls*
*Fat per roll—0.26 g.*

# Chocolate-Cherry Bread

The addition of cocoa adds richness and complexity to this bread, not sweetness. It's a singular dinner bread with a heartiness and texture seldom found in nonyeast breads.

¼ pound dried sour cherries
¼ cup boiling water
1¼ cups medium rye flour
1¾ cups plus ½ teaspoon all-purpose flour
1½ teaspoons baking powder
1 teaspoon baking soda
1 teaspoon salt
3 tablespoons unsweetened
  Dutch-processed cocoa powder

3 tablespoons nonfat liquid egg substitute
¼ cup honey
2 tablespoons natural unsweetened
  applesauce
¾ teaspoon vanilla extract
1 cup buttermilk
1 tablespoon cornmeal

Preheat the oven to 375 degrees.

Mix the cherries and boiling water in a small bowl and set aside.

Sift the rye flour, 1½ cups of the all-purpose flour, the baking powder, baking soda, salt, and cocoa powder together into a large mixing bowl.

In a separate bowl, beat the liquid egg substitute until frothy with an electric mixer. Add the honey, applesauce, vanilla extract, and buttermilk. Beat to mix.

Add the egg mixture to the flour mixture and blend with a wooden spoon just until the flour is absorbed. Drain the cherries and stir them into the mixture. Sprinkle ¼ cup of all-purpose flour over the top and work by hand into a dough ball. Let the dough sit in the bowl for 5 minutes.

Transfer the dough to a nonstick cookie sheet sprinkled with the cornmeal. Using a sieve, dust the top of the dough with the remaining ½ teaspoon flour. With a sharp knife that has been dipped in flour, cut an "X" in the center of the bread.

Bake for 40 to 50 minutes, until a tester inserted into the center comes out clean.

Yield—12 slices
Fat per slice—0.61 g.

# Orange-Bran Muffins

2 cups all-purpose flour
2½ teaspoons baking powder
1 teaspoon baking soda
¼ teaspoon salt
½ teaspoon ground cloves
½ teaspoon ground nutmeg
¼ teaspoon ground cinnamon
¾ cup honey
1½ cups orange juice

2 cups oat bran
¼ cup buttermilk
¼ cup dark unsulphured molasses
¾ cup peeled, shredded carrot
   (1–2 carrots)
¾ cup golden raisins
¼ cup plain nonfat yogurt
Light vegetable oil cooking spray

Preheat the oven to 375 degrees.

Sift the flour, baking powder, baking soda, salt, and spices together and set aside.

Whisk the honey and orange juice to blend. Add the oat bran and whisk thoroughly.

Combine the buttermilk and molasses in a large mixing bowl and whisk well. Thoroughly mix in the carrot, then the oat bran mixture.

Add the raisins to the flour mixture and stir into the oat bran–buttermilk mixture with a wooden spoon. Fold in the yogurt.

Spray vegetable oil spray over the surface of 12 large muffin tin cups for about 3 seconds, covering as much of the exposed surface as possible. Spread the oil evenly into the wells with your fingers. Fill the wells to the top with batter. Bake for 25 to 30 minutes, until a tester inserted into the center of a muffin comes out clean.

*Yield — 12 oversized muffins*
*Fat per muffin — 0.83 g.*

In this recipe, we use a baker's paper liner to eliminate the need to oil the loaf pan to prevent sticking. The paper liners are available in most kitchenware stores.

# Good Morning Zucchini Muffins

2 cups all-purpose flour
2 teaspoons baking powder
¼ teaspoon baking soda
½ teaspoon salt
6 tablespoons nonfat liquid egg substitute
1 teaspoon grated orange rind
⅓ cup light corn syrup
6 tablespoons dark brown sugar,
   firmly packed

½ teaspoon ground allspice
1¼ teaspoons ground cinnamon
¼ teaspoon ground cloves
1 cup peeled, shredded zucchini
   (about 12 ounces)
½ cup seedless raisins
Light vegetable oil cooking spray

Preheat the oven to 400 degrees.

Sift the flour, baking powder, baking soda, and salt together and set aside.

Put the egg substitute into a large mixing bowl and whisk for about 30 seconds, until frothy. Whisk in the orange rind and corn syrup. Add the sugar and spices and whisk. Whisk in the zucchini, then the raisins.

Dump this into the flour mixture and combine with a wooden spoon, just until blended.

Spray the vegetable oil spray over the surface of 12 muffin tin cups for about 3 seconds, covering as much of the exposed surface as possible. Spread the oil evenly into the wells with your fingers. Fill the wells about two-thirds full with batter. Bake for 15 minutes, until the muffins begin to separate from the sides of the tin and a tester inserted into the center of a muffin comes out clean.

Store in an airtight container.

*Yield—12 muffins*
*Fat per muffin—0.47 g.*

# Banana Tea Bread

2 cups all-purpose flour
½ teaspoon baking soda
2 teaspoons baking powder
½ teaspoon salt
1¼ teaspoons ground cinnamon
¼ teaspoon ground nutmeg
⅛ teaspoon ground allspice

2 large eggs, whites only
⅔ cup buttermilk
⅔ cup light brown sugar, firmly packed
1 teaspoon vanilla extract
1⅓ cups mashed very ripe banana
   (3–4 bananas)
¼ cup light corn syrup

Preheat the oven to 375 degrees.

Sift the flour, baking soda, baking powder, salt, and spices together and set aside.

In a large mixing bowl, combine the egg whites and ⅓ cup of the buttermilk. Beat with an electric mixer at high speed for about 2 minutes, until frothy. At low speed, beat in the remaining ⅓ cup of buttermilk, the brown sugar, and the vanilla extract. Beat in the banana until well blended, then the corn syrup. Add the dry ingredients and mix with a wooden spoon just until blended.

Insert a paper liner into an 8½-inch loaf pan and pour in the batter. Bake for about 50 minutes, until the edges of the loaf begin to separate from the pan and a tester inserted into the center of the loaf comes out clean.

*Yield — 16 slices*
*Fat per slice — 0.32 g.*

# Strawberry-Apple Quick Bread

1½ cups all-purpose flour
2 teaspoons baking powder
½ teaspoon salt
½ cup sugar
½ cup natural unsweetened applesauce
6 tablespoons nonfat strawberry yogurt
1 teaspoon vanilla extract

1½ teaspoons ground cinnamon
¼ teaspoon ground nutmeg
¼ cup dark brown sugar, firmly packed
¼ cup rolled oats
1¼ cups mashed very ripe banana (about 3 medium bananas)

Preheat the oven to 375 degrees.

Sift the flour, baking powder, salt, and sugar together into a bowl.

In a large mixing bowl, combine the applesauce and yogurt. Add the vanilla, cinnamon, and nutmeg, mixing well. Beat in the brown sugar. Stir in the oats. Add the banana and mix well. Add the flour mixture and blend well with a wooden spoon.

Pour the batter into a nonstick 9¼-inch loaf pan. Bake for 40 to 50 minutes, until the loaf begins to separate from the edges of the pan and a tester inserted in the center comes out clean. Remove from the oven, cool a few minutes in the pan, then turn the loaf out onto a rack.

*Yield—16 slices*
*Fat per slice—0.27 g.*

# Skillet Corn Bread

1⅓ cups yellow cornmeal
⅔ cup all-purpose flour
1 teaspoon baking powder
1 teaspoon baking soda
1 teaspoon salt
1½ cups buttermilk

¼ cup light corn syrup
2 tablespoons skim milk
5 tablespoons plain nonfat yogurt
2 large eggs, whites only
Light vegetable oil cooking spray

In this recipe, we have removed the fat from our favorite corn bread—a light, fluffy version with a crusty bottom derived from skillet baking.

Put a large, heavy, well-seasoned cast-iron skillet into an oven pre-heated to 450 degrees.

Sift the dry ingredients together into a large mixing bowl. Set aside.

In another bowl, whisk together the buttermilk and corn syrup until well blended and frothy. Add the skim milk and whisk again. Whisk in the yogurt until just dissolved.

Beat the egg whites with an electric mixer until they form stiff peaks.

Pour the buttermilk mixture into the flour and blend well, using a wooden spoon. Gently fold in the beaten egg whites.

Remove the skillet from the oven and spray it 3 times lightly with vegetable oil spray. Pour in the batter, return the pan to the oven, and bake the corn bread for about 15 minutes, until the edges brown. Serve immediately.

*Yield—10 wedges*
*Fat per wedge—0.87 g.*

*8*

# DESSERTS

# Flourless Chocolate Cake

2 ounces whole dried apricots
   (about 6 apricots)
½ cup cold water
¼ cup boiling water
8 large eggs, whites only (do not combine)

1 cup sugar
½ cup unsweetened Dutch-processed
   cocoa powder
1 cup Grape-Nuts cereal
Light vegetable oil cooking spray

Preheat the oven to 350 degrees.

Combine the dried apricots and the cold water in a small saucepan and bring to a boil over medium heat. Cover, reduce the heat to low, and simmer for 20 minutes.

Remove from the heat and pour into the bowl of a food processor or blender. Add the boiling water and puree until smooth. (You should have about 3 tablespoons of apricot puree.)

Combine the puree, 2 of the egg whites, the sugar, and the cocoa powder in a large mixing bowl. Whisk together well. Add the Grape-Nuts and mix with a wooden spoon.

Using an electric mixer (preferably the heavy, stationary type), beat the 6 remaining egg whites at medium speed until they form stiff, dry peaks.

Add a third of the beaten egg whites to the apricot-cocoa mixture and stir with a wooden spoon until thoroughly incorporated. Add the remaining egg whites. Fold gently with a slotted spoon until completely incorporated.

Spray the bottom and sides of a 9-inch springform pan once lightly with the vegetable oil spray. Spread the oil evenly over the surface of the pan with your fingers.

Slowly pour in the batter, shaking the pan gently to even the top. Bake for about 25 minutes, until the cake is firm to the touch in the center and the sides begin to pull away from the pan.

Remove from the oven, place the pan on a rack, and cool thoroughly. The cake will shrink some as it cools.

*Yield — 10 servings*
*Fat per serving — 0.65 g.*

This is an elegant finale to the most stylish of meals, one that will humble more fatty desserts by comparison. Don't be put off by the use of Grape-Nuts, which provide all the taste and texture of real nuts with none of the guilt. Keep in mind that the trick to making this flourless cake is taking care not to overbeat the egg whites.

Let the cake stand on its own: Finish it with a sprinkling of powdered sugar, or fan a strawberry on each slice. We also like it topped with the Roasted Banana Sauce or Mixed Berry Sauce (page 177 or 180).

# Pumpkin Swirl Cheesecake

The eye-catching swirl will add a festive accent to your dessert board. This cheesecake derives its buttery texture from the inclusion of pumpkin puree.

*CRUST:*
1¼ cups rolled oats
2 tablespoons dark brown sugar, firmly packed
2 tablespoons all-purpose flour
¼ cup pear nectar
Light vegetable oil cooking spray

*FILLING:*
1½ cups Yogurt Cheese (see Pantry)
¼ cup plain nonfat yogurt
¾ cup granulated sugar
1 teaspoon vanilla extract
6 tablespoons nonfat liquid egg substitute
1 teaspoon Frangelico liqueur
1 cup pumpkin puree
¾ teaspoon ground cinnamon
¼ teaspoon ground nutmeg

Preheat the oven to 350 degrees.

To make the crust, combine the rolled oats, brown sugar, flour, and pear nectar and mix well.

Lightly spray a 9-inch springform pan once with the vegetable oil spray and evenly distribute it with your fingers over the inner surface of the pan. Scrape the batter (which will be very thick) into the pan. Pat the top to even it, by hand or using the back of a soup spoon, and bake for 15 minutes. Remove from the oven to cool. Leave the oven on.

For the cake, using an electric mixer at medium speed, beat the yogurt cheese, yogurt, ½ cup of the sugar, and the vanilla extract until well blended. Add the egg substitute, 2 tablespoons at a time, mixing well after each addition. Remove 1 cup of the mixture and set aside.

To the mixing bowl, add the remaining ¼ cup of granulated sugar, the Frangelico, pumpkin puree, and the spices. Mix well with an electric mixer until all the ingredients are well incorporated.

Pour atop one side of the crust. Pour the reserved cup of yogurt mixture on the other side. Shake lightly to even the top. With a dinner knife, cut through both batters several times in a circular motion to create a marbleized effect. Bake for 1 hour, until firm.

Remove from the oven and place on a rack. Run a knife around the sides of the pan to loosen the cake. Cool for 30 to 40 minutes in the pan, then remove the sides. Chill in the refrigerator for 2 to 3 hours before serving.

*Yield — 12 servings*
*Fat per serving — 0.77 g.*

# Cocoa Cheesecake

This is a very special chocolate treat. Most people we've served it to have been so intrigued by the notion that a dessert with this intense chocolate flavor can be virtually fat free that they don't even notice the more basic alchemy at work here—the substitution of Yogurt Cheese for cream cheese and sour cream in the base.

*CRUST:*

3 tablespoons light corn syrup
¼ cup sugar
3 tablespoons nonfat liquid egg substitute
⅔ cup all-purpose flour
1½ tablespoons unsweetened Dutch-
    processed cocoa powder
Light vegetable oil cooking spray

*FILLING:*

½ cup dried apple chunks
    (about 2 ounces)
⅓ cup cold water
10 tablespoons boiling water
¼ cup light corn syrup
¾ cup unsweetened Dutch-processed
    cocoa powder
1¾ cups Yogurt Cheese (see Pantry)
⅔ cup sugar
6 tablespoons nonfat liquid egg substitute
½ tablespoon vanilla extract

Preheat the oven to 450 degrees.

To make the crust, beat the corn syrup and sugar with an electric mixer until the sugar is dissolved and the mixture is slightly frothy. Beat in the egg substitute.

Add the flour and cocoa powder. Mix well with a wooden spoon.

Spray a 9-inch springform pan once lightly with vegetable oil spray and evenly distribute the oil around the inside surface of the pan with your fingers.

Scrape the batter (which will be very thick) evenly into the pan with a spatula. Bake for 10 minutes and remove from the oven.

Lower the oven temperature to 350 degrees.

For the filling, bring the dried apple and cold water to a boil in a small saucepan. Cover, lower the heat, and simmer for 20 minutes.

Transfer to a food processor or blender and puree while slowly adding 6 tablespoons of the boiling water.

Place 6 tablespoons of the puree into a bowl (discard any left over). Add the corn syrup and cocoa powder. Mix well. Continue to mix while adding the remaining 4 tablespoons boiling water. The mixture should be smooth and glossy, resembling melted chocolate. Set it aside.

In another bowl, combine the yogurt cheese and the sugar. Using an electric mixer, beat at medium speed until well blended. Add the liquid egg substitute, 2 tablespoons at a time, beating well after each addition.

Scrape in the chocolate mixture and add the vanilla extract. Blend well with a spatula. Pour into the crust. Bake for 45 minutes, until firm.

Remove from the oven and place on a rack. Run a dinner knife around the sides of the pan to loosen the cake. Cool for 30 to 40 minutes in the pan, then remove the sides and chill in the refrigerator for at least 2 hours before serving.

*Yield — 12 servings*
*Fat per serving — 0.40 g.*

# Individual Peach and Sour Cherry Strudel

This is best made in late summer, when the peaches are at their prime. The quality of this strudel is truly dependent on the quality of the peaches used. You can, however, substitute natural unsweetened peach nectar for the juice component if you don't have an extractor. For an added touch, spoon a little Cinnamon Cream Topping (page 179) over the strudel.

*4 ripe peaches (about 22 ounces total), halved and stoned*
*6 tablespoons granulated sugar*
*2 tablespoons ground cinnamon*

*6 sheets phyllo dough (about 4½ ounces)*
*¼ cup dried sour cherries*
*1 teaspoon confectioners sugar*

Preheat the oven to 450 degrees.

Put 2 peaches through a juice extractor. (This should yield about ½ cup juice.)

Cut the remaining peaches lengthwise into ¼-inch slices.

Combine the sugar and cinnamon in a small bowl.

Layer 3 sheets of phyllo dough on top of each other, painting the top of each one with peach juice as you assemble them. Sprinkle about half the sugar and cinnamon mixture over the top sheet. Layer another 3 sheets, painting between them but not on top of the last sheet. Sprinkle with the remaining sugar and cinnamon.

Cut the layered sheets into quarters. Mound an equal amount of peaches along one short side of each quarter, leaving an exposed border on 3 sides. Spoon 1 tablespoon of dried cherries over and alongside the peaches. Raise the border next to the filling and roll the dough continuously over onto itself to form a log. Crimp the open ends to seal.

Transfer the logs to a parchment-lined baking sheet and brush the exposed dough with peach juice. Bake for about 6 minutes, until the logs are golden brown.

Remove from the oven. With a serrated knife, trim the crimped ends to expose the filling and sprinkle the tops with the confectioners sugar.

*Yield—4 servings*
*Fat per serving—0.65 g.*

# Banana-Chocolate Rice Pudding

One 8-ounce banana, unpeeled
6 tablespoons nonfat liquid egg substitute
⅔ cup buttermilk
1 tablespoon unsweetened Dutch-processed
   cocoa powder

¼ cup light brown sugar, firmly packed
½ teaspoon vanilla extract
1 cup cooked white rice, packed
Light vegetable oil cooking spray

Preheat the oven to 350 degrees.

Put the banana in the oven and roast for about 15 minutes, until it turns black and soft.

Remove the banana and lower the oven temperature to 325 degrees.

Let the banana sit until cool enough to handle. Peel, transfer the flesh to a small bowl, and mash it with a fork. Set aside.

Put the egg substitute into a mixing bowl and whisk until frothy. Whisk in the buttermilk. Add the cocoa powder, brown sugar, vanilla extract, mashed banana, and cooked rice, whisking after each addition.

Spray a 1-quart glass casserole once lightly with vegetable oil spray, and distribute the oil evenly over the surface. Transfer the pudding mixture to the casserole and bake for 45 minutes.

Remove the pudding from the oven and let it sit for about 10 minutes before serving. The pudding can be served warm or at room temperature.

*Yield—4 servings*
*Fat per serving—0.90 g.*

The richness in this version of the traditional rice pudding is derived from banana and buttermilk instead of butter and cream. Warm, succulent, and good for the soul.

# Apple Upside-Down Cake

This recipe is a fat-free rendition of a wonderful Rosh Hashanah cake created by our friend Jill Van Cleave for her Chicago bakery. It's a very moist cake that stands on its own but also works well with Cinnamon Cream Topping (page 179).

¼ cup honey
¼ cup dark brown sugar, firmly packed
2 Granny Smith apples (about 1 pound total), peeled, cored, and cut into ¼-inch slices (should yield about 2½ cups sliced apples)
Light vegetable oil cooking spray
¾ cup granulated sugar
½ cup light corn syrup

1 large egg, white only
1 cup natural unsweetened applesauce
½ cup buttermilk
1 teaspoon baking soda
1½ teaspoons ground cinnamon
¼ teaspoon freshly grated nutmeg
½ teaspoon salt
2¼ cups all-purpose flour

Preheat the oven to 350 degrees.

Combine the honey and brown sugar in a nonstick frying pan. Cook over medium heat until the sugar dissolves, 2 to 3 minutes. Add the apples and continue to cook for about 4 minutes, stirring often, until the apples begin to soften. Remove from the heat.

Wrap the bottom and outer sides of a 9-inch springform pan with aluminum foil. Lightly spray the inside surface once with vegetable oil spray, distributing the oil evenly with your fingers. Transfer the apple mixture to the pan and arrange the slices into an even layer on the bottom.

Put the granulated sugar and corn syrup into a large bowl and beat with an electric mixer at medium speed until blended. Add the egg white and beat at high speed until the mixture is smooth. Beat in the applesauce and buttermilk and continue beating at high speed for 1 minute. The mixture should have a slight froth.

Combine the remaining ingredients then add to the batter in the large bowl and mix until smooth.

Spread the batter evenly over the apples. Place the pan on a baking sheet and bake on the middle rack of the oven for 40 to 45 minutes, until a tester inserted into the center of the cake's top comes out clean.

Remove from the oven and cool in the pan, on a rack, for 15 minutes. Run a dinner knife around the inner edges of the pan and invert the cake onto a serving platter. Replace any apple slices that may have dislodged from the top of the cake.

*Yield — 10 servings*
*Fat per serving — 0.61 g.*

# Linzertorte

We have substituted apricot for the more traditional raspberry filling, because it provides a nice, smooth contrast to the nutty texture of the dough. The torte can be served individually in wedges, or chilled and sliced as you would a bar cookie for a buffet presentation.

1¼ cups Grape-Nuts cereal
1½ cups all-purpose flour
¾ cup granulated sugar
1 teaspoon ground cinnamon
¼ teaspoon ground cloves
1¼ teaspoons baking powder
¾ cup natural unsweetened applesauce
3 tablespoons plain nonfat yogurt

Light vegetable oil cooking spray
⅞ cup apricot spreadable fruit
   (about one 10-ounce jar)
1 large egg, white only
1 teaspoon skim milk
½ teaspoon confectioners sugar,
   for topping

Put the cereal into the bowl of a food processor or blender and process to the consistency of finely ground nuts.

Transfer to a large mixing bowl. Add the dry ingredients. Mix together with a fork, making sure to blend well. Add the applesauce and yogurt. Stir until the mixture is smooth and all the dry ingredients have been incorporated. Form into a ball by hand, enclose the dough in plastic wrap, and refrigerate for 1 hour.

Preheat the oven to 350 degrees.

Spray the bottom of a 9-inch springform pan once lightly with the vegetable oil spray and distribute the oil evenly over the surface of the pan with your fingers.

Remove the dough from the refrigerator and cut it in half. Place half the dough in the pan and press it out evenly to cover the entire bottom surface. Cover the dough evenly with the spreadable fruit, leaving a ½-inch border.

Cut the remaining dough into long thin slices. Lightly flour your hands and work each slice into a thin cigar-shaped rope. Lay 4 evenly spaced ropes in each direction across the top of the spreadable fruit in a lattice pattern. Work any excess dough into a long rope to encircle the outer border (This border can be made up of shorter dough ropes crimped together.)

Mix the egg white and skim milk together well. Using a pastry brush, paint the exposed surface of the dough with the mixture.

Bake for 35 to 40 minutes, until the dough is uniformly golden brown and firm to the touch. Transfer to a rack and cool in the pan. Remove the sides and sift the confectioners sugar over the top of the torte.

*Yield — 10 servings*
*Fat per serving — 0.27 g.*

This is based on a recipe from World War II, when eggs and butter were hard to come by. The holes poked in the cake before glazing allow the topping to penetrate, adding moisture and a pervading lemon aroma. Apply the glaze repeatedly, allowing the cake to absorb the liquid between each application.

# Spice Cake with Lemon Glaze

*SPICE CAKE:*
*2 cups boiling water*
*1 cup dried currants*
*2½ cups all-purpose flour*
*6 tablespoons cornstarch*
*2 teaspoons baking soda*
*1 teaspoon baking powder*
*1½ teaspoons ground cinnamon*
*1 teaspoon ground allspice*
*½ teaspoon ground cloves*
*½ teaspoon salt*
*1½ cups dark brown sugar, firmly packed*
*⅔ cup light corn syrup*
*2 teaspoons vanilla extract*
*2 tablespoons freshly squeezed lemon juice*
*Light vegetable oil cooking spray*

*LEMON GLAZE:*
*1 cup plain nonfat yogurt*
*1 cup confectioners sugar*
*2 teaspoons freshly squeezed lemon juice*

Preheat the oven to 350 degrees.

For the cake, mix the boiling water and currants in a small bowl and set aside.

Sift flour, cornstarch, baking soda, baking powder, and spices together.

Cream the brown sugar, corn syrup, vanilla extract, and lemon juice in a large mixing bowl, using a wire whisk.

Whisk in about a third of the dry ingredients, then half of the water-currant mixture. Whisk in another third of the dry ingredients, followed by the remainder of the water-currant mixture and, finally, the remaining third of the dry ingredients.

Lightly spray a 12-cup tube pan once with the vegetable oil spray, spreading the oil evenly over the inside surface with your fingers. Pour in the batter.

Bake for 45 to 50 minutes, until a tester comes out clean. Cool for 10 minutes in the pan on a rack. Run a dinner knife around the edges of the cake to loosen it. Remove the cake from the pan, set it on a rack, and prick a number of holes in the top and sides with a toothpick.

Combine all the glaze ingredients and mix with a whisk until smooth and blended.

Spread some of the glaze evenly over the top of the cake, allowing it to drip down the sides. Periodically add more glaze as the cake cools.

*Yield — 24 servings*
*Fat per serving — 0.17 g.*

# Persimmon Mousse

The "late-blooming" persimmon has lent a hint of summer-past to many a year-end meal. Just when it seems the harvest is long gone, this refreshing fruit comes into season.

1 pound ripe persimmon (about 2 large persimmons), trimmed and peeled
¼ cup granulated sugar
2 tablespoons unflavored gelatin (1 packet)

¼ cup water
1 teaspoon plus 2 tablespoons light rum
½ cup evaporated skim milk, well chilled
2 tablespoons confectioners sugar

Puree the persimmon in a food processor or blender to a smooth consistency. (You should have about 1½ cups puree.)

Put the granulated sugar and gelatin in a small saucepan. Stir in the water and let sit for 1 minute. Turn on low heat and cook for about 3 minutes, stirring constantly, until the sugar and gelatin have completely dissolved. Remove from the heat.

Combine the gelatin mixture with 1 cup of the persimmon puree and 1 teaspoon of the rum in a bowl and stir to blend completely. Cover tightly and refrigerate until chilled and thick, about 45 minutes. When you put this mixture into the refrigerator, place a metal mixing bowl and the beaters from an electric mixer into the freezer.

After 45 minutes, put the evaporated milk into the chilled bowl. Beat on high with the chilled beaters just until stiff (taking care not to overbeat). Beat in the chilled mixture, and spoon into 4-ounce parfait glasses.

For the sauce, mix the remaining ½ cup of persimmon puree with the 2 tablespoons rum and the confectioners sugar. Spoon a little over each serving.

*Yield—6 servings*
*Fat per serving—0.28 g.*

# Poached Pears
## with Port Sauce

For variety, we sometimes replace the port sauce with Mixed Berry Sauce (page 180).

### POACHED PEARS:
1 cup white wine
⅔ cup water
⅓ cup sugar
2½ ounces navel orange, peeled, seeded, and thinly sliced
6 firm Bartlett pears (about 2½ pounds total), peeled, stems left intact
2 tablespoons freshly grated ginger

### PORT SAUCE:
3 tablespoons port wine
½ cup plain nonfat yogurt

To poach the pears, combine the wine, water, and sugar in a large saucepan or pot. Bring to a boil over medium heat, reduce the heat, and simmer for 5 minutes. Add the orange slices, pears and ginger. Cover partially and cook for 45 minutes to 1 hour, until the pears are fork tender.

Remove from the heat and allow the pears to cool in the pan. Transfer the cooled pears to a bowl and pour the poaching liquid on top. Cover and refrigerate for 2 to 3 hours, until well chilled.

For the sauce, whisk the port into the yogurt until well blended.

To serve, roll each pear in the chilled poaching liquid just to coat it and transfer with a slotted spoon to a small plate. (The pear should stand upright on the plate.) Top with a little sauce and serve immediately.

*Yield — 6 servings*
*Fat per serving — 0.73 g.*

# Chocolate-Hazelnut Biscotti

The classic Italian dunking cookie. The last step of the recipe should really be to submerge the biscotti briefly into a steaming cup of espresso or cappuccino.

½ cup honey
1 tablespoon instant coffee granules
½ cup granulated sugar
½ cup dark brown sugar, firmly packed
¼ cup Frangelico liqueur
10 tablespoons nonfat liquid egg
   substitute

3 cups all-purpose flour, plus a little
   extra for flouring during preparation
⅓ cup unsweetened Dutch-processed
   cocoa powder
2 teaspoons baking powder
¼ teaspoon salt

Preheat the oven to 350 degrees.

Put the honey and coffee granules in a small saucepan and warm for about 2 minutes over low heat, until the granules dissolve. (Or combine in a small bowl and microwave for about 20 seconds at full power.)

In a large mixing bowl, combine the coffee mixture with the sugars, liqueur, and egg substitute. Whisk until well blended. Sift the remaining ingredients together into the mixture. Stir to combine thoroughly.

Turn the dough out onto a lightly floured surface and gently knead for about 30 seconds, until the dough holds together. Work it into a loaf about 16 inches long by 4 inches wide. Place the loaf on a baking sheet lined with baker's parchment, and bake for about 25 minutes, until firm.

Remove from the oven and lower the temperature to 275 degrees.

Transfer the loaf to a rack and cool for 15 minutes, then put it on a cutting board. Using a serrated knife, cut the loaf into ½-inch slices on the diagonal. Remove the parchment from the cookie sheet and place the slices on the sheet, with one of the cut sides of each slice exposed. Bake for 30 to 35 minutes, turning after 15 minutes to expose the other cut side of each slice. The biscotti should be done when they look dry and toasted. Remove from the oven and allow to cool and crisp.

*Yield — 22 biscotti*
*Fat per biscotti — 0.27 g.*

# Orange-Buttermilk Ice Cream

This is our updated rendition of the traditional Pennsylvania Dutch buttermilk ice cream. We suggest pairing it with either the chilled Mixed Berry Sauce or the warm Rum-Raisin Sauce (page 180 or 178).

*2 cups buttermilk*
*⅓ cup confectioners sugar*

*1 tablespoon Triple Sec liqueur*

Combine the buttermilk and sugar and beat with an electric mixer until the sugar has dissolved and the mixture is frothy. Beat in the liqueur. Chill for 1 hour in the freezer.

Process in an ice cream maker according to the manufacturer's instructions.

*Yield — 4 servings*
*Fat per serving — 1.0 g.*

# Champagne Sorbet with Apricot Sauce

### CHAMPAGNE SORBET:
2 cups water
1 cup sugar
1 cup brut champagne

### APRICOT SAUCE:
6 medium apricots (about 8 ounces total)
1 teaspoon freshly squeezed lemon juice
2 teaspoons sugar

To make the sorbet, combine the water and the sugar in a saucepan and bring to a boil over medium heat. Lower the heat and simmer for 5 minutes. Remove from the heat, stir in the champagne, and cool to room temperature. Allow to chill in the refrigerator for 1 hour, then process in an ice cream maker according to the manufacturer's instructions.

To make the sauce, bring a large saucepan or pot of water to a boil. Make an "X" on the skin of each apricot. Drop the apricots into the boiling water and bring back to a boil. Remove and peel, pit, and chop the apricots.

Combine the chopped apricots, lemon juice, and sugar in a food processor and puree until smooth.

Serve a heaping scoop of sorbet either set on top of the sauce or with the sauce drizzled over and around the sorbet.

*Yield — 6 servings*
*Fat per serving — 0.10 g.*

A light and refreshing palate cleanser that is the perfect thing to serve after such hearty dishes as chili or gumbo. We suggest preparing it a couple of hours in advance (or the day before serving) and storing it in the freezer, because homemade sorbets and ice creams that include alcohol usually take longer to solidify. The thick apricot sauce can be spooned onto the dessert plate as a base or drizzled over the sorbet.

# Honeydew Granita with Melon Balls

A novel change from the more common smooth sorbet, this frozen dessert has a coarse, granular texture. We've found it to be a memorable way to conclude a long, leisurely brunch.

*One 4-pound honeydew melon*
*2 tablespoons freshly squeezed lemon juice*

*2 tablespoons chopped fresh mint, plus 4 sprigs for garnish*

Remove the rind and seeds from the melon. Cube about half (to yield 3 cups cubed melon) and reserve the rest.

Combine the cubed honeydew, lemon juice, and chopped mint in a food processor or blender and puree until very smooth. Transfer to a bowl and freeze for 3 hours.

Scoop 20 honeydew balls from the reserved melon with a melon-ball cutter. Remove the granita from the freezer and chop it into rough crystals.

Place 5 honeydew balls in each of 4 balloon glasses. Top with granita and garnish with a sprig of mint.

*Yield—4 servings*
*Fat per serving—0.15 g.*

# Lemon Madeleines

1 large egg, white only
2½ tablespoons sugar
1 tablespoon light corn syrup

1½ tablespoons all-purpose flour
1 teaspoon finely grated lemon rind
Light vegetable oil cooking spray

Preheat the oven to 350 degrees.

Put the egg white into a mixing bowl and beat until frothy. Add the sugar and corn syrup. Stir in the flour and lemon rind, mixing until completely blended.

Lightly spray vegetable oil twice on a madeleine tin, and distribute it evenly over the surface of the molds using your fingers. Scoop 1 tablespoon of batter into each mold. Bake for about 11 minutes, until the edges of the cakes are golden brown.

Place a sheet of baker's parchment on top of a wire rack. Remove the madeleine tin from the oven, invert, and lightly tap to release the madeleines onto the parchment to cool. Serve the same day.

*Yield — 6 madeleines*
*Fat per madeleine — 0.35 g.*

This simple version of the small French sponge cake is a smashing accompaniment to the Honeydew Granita (see page 168). Madeleine tins are available from most kitchenware stores.

# Ginger Madeleines

We like to serve ginger madeleines with Champagne Sorbet (page 167).

2½ tablespoons sugar
1 tablespoon light corn syrup
1 large egg, white only, beaten until
  frothy

1½ tablespoons all-purpose flour
1 teaspoon grated fresh ginger
Light vegetable oil cooking spray

Preheat the oven to 350 degrees.

Add the sugar and corn syrup to the beaten egg white. Stir in the flour and ginger until completely blended.

Lightly spray vegetable oil twice on a madeleine tin, spreading it into all the crevices of the molds with your fingers. Scoop 1 tablespoon of batter into each mold. Bake for about 11 minutes, until the edges of the cakes are golden brown.

Remove from the oven and invert the madeleines onto a sheet of baker's parchment set atop a cooling rack. Serve the same day.

*Yield—6 madeleines*
*Fat per madeleine—0.35 g.*

# Chocolate-Apricot Madeleines

1 ounce whole dried apricots
   (about 3 apricots)
¼ cup cold water
2 tablespoons boiling water
1 large egg, white only

3 tablespoons sugar
1 teaspoon unsweetened Dutch-processed
   cocoa powder
1½ tablespoons all-purpose flour

Preheat the oven to 350 degrees.

Combine the dried apricots and the cold water in a small saucepan and bring to a boil over medium heat. Cover, reduce the heat to low, and simmer for 20 minutes.

Remove from the heat and pour into the bowl of a food processor or blender. Add the boiling water and puree until smooth.

Put the egg white into a mixing bowl and beat until frothy. Add the sugar and 1 tablespoon of the apricot puree (discard any left over). Stir in the cocoa powder and flour, mixing until completely blended.

Lightly spray the vegetable oil twice on a madeleine tin, and spread it evenly over the surface of the molds using your fingers. Scoop 1 tablespoon of batter into each mold. Bake until the edges of the cakes are golden brown, about 11 minutes.

Place a sheet of baker's parchment on top of a wire rack. Remove the tin from the oven, invert, and lightly tap to release the madeleines onto the parchment to cool. Serve the same day.

*Yield — 6 madeleines*
*Fat per madeleine — 0.41 g.*

Great with the Orange-Buttermilk Ice Cream (page 166). Serve the pale ice cream in a balloon glass, with a dark, rich madeleine impaled on the rim for a striking visual contrast.

# Strawberry-Rhubarb Crumble

This is a fat-free comfort food, similar to an old-fashioned Brown Betty. Bake in a casserole, rather than in a broader, shallower baking dish, if you like a thicker layer of crumble on top of each portion.

2 ounces whole dried apricots
   (about 6 apricots)
½ cup cold water
¼ cup boiling water
½ cup all-purpose flour
¼ cup dark brown sugar, firmly packed
¼ cup granulated sugar
¼ teaspoon salt
⅛ teaspoon ground ginger
⅛ teaspoon freshly grated nutmeg

FILLING:
1 pound firm fresh rhubarb
12 ounces strawberries, hulled
⅓ cup granulated sugar
3 tablespoons all-purpose flour
½ teaspoon grated lemon rind

Preheat the oven to 400 degrees.

For the crumble, combine the dried apricots and the cold water in a small saucepan and bring to a boil over medium heat. Cover, reduce the heat to low, and simmer for 20 minutes.

Remove from the heat and pour into the bowl of a food processor or blender. Add the boiling water and puree until smooth. (You should have about 3 tablespoons apricot puree.)

Combine the remaining dry ingredients in a bowl and mix thoroughly. Add the apricot puree and mix with a fork to the texture of coarse meal. Set aside.

For the filling, trim the rhubarb and cut it into ¼-inch chunks. Put the chunks into a 1-quart casserole or an 8-by-8-inch nonstick baking pan. Cut the strawberries in half and add to the rhubarb. Add the sugar, flour, and lemon rind and mix thoroughly with a spatula.

Sprinkle the crumble over the fruit filling and bake for 25 to 30 minutes, until the top is browned and the edges are bubbly. Remove from the oven and let sit for 10 minutes before serving.

*Yield—4 servings*
*Fat per serving—0.71 g.*

# Soft Chewy Oatmeal Cookies

1½ cups rolled oats
1 cup all-purpose flour
½ teaspoon baking soda
½ teaspoon baking powder
½ teaspoon salt
¾ cup natural unsweetened applesauce

½ cup dark brown sugar, firmly packed
¼ cup light corn syrup
1 large egg, white only, beaten
1 teaspoon vanilla extract
¾ teaspoon ground cinnamon
1 cup seedless raisins

Preheat the oven to 350 degrees.

Put the oats, flour, baking soda, baking powder, and salt into a bowl, mix thoroughly, and set aside.

In a large mixing bowl, combine the applesauce, brown sugar, and corn syrup. Mix until the sugar is completely dissolved. Stir in the beaten egg white, then the vanilla extract. Add the cinnamon and the rolled oat mixture. Stir well. Fold in the raisins.

With a ¼-cup measure, scoop level measures of dough onto an ungreased cookie sheet, leaving 2 inches of space between each. Bake for about 15 minutes, until the edges turn golden brown.

Remove the cookie sheet from the oven and cool for about 1 minute, then transfer the cookies to a rack and cool for 10 to 15 minutes longer.

*Yield—Fourteen 3½-inch cookies*
*Fat per cookie—0.55 g.*

We created this fat-free goodie in response to the challenge set down by our literary agent, Susan Ramer, who has very demanding standards for "the perfect oatmeal cookie." It wasn't easy, but Susan says we succeeded.

# Old-Fashioned Cocoa Brownies

The all-time ultimate, moist, chewy, chocolate brownie, with a minuscule fraction of the fat found in any other brownie. Treat the yogurt as if it were egg white, gently folding, rather than stirring it into the batter.

*1 cup unsweetened Dutch-processed cocoa powder*
*¾ teaspoon baking soda*
*½ teaspoon salt*
*½ cup double-strength hot brewed coffee*
*¼ cup light corn syrup*

*1 cup natural unsweetened applesauce*
*2 cups sugar*
*1 teaspoon vanilla extract*
*1½ cups all-purpose flour*
*½ cup plain nonfat yogurt*

Preheat the oven to 350 degrees.

Sift the cocoa powder, baking soda, and salt together into a large bowl. Add the coffee and corn syrup. Blend with a wire whisk until the mixture is smooth and glossy. Add the applesauce, sugar, and vanilla extract. Whisk until completely blended. Add the flour. Fold in the yogurt with a wooden spoon just until it is incorporated.

Fold the batter into an 8-by-8-inch nonstick baking pan. Bake for about 30 minutes, until the mixture is just beginning to separate from the edges of the pan and is firm to the touch in the center.

Remove from the oven, place on a rack, and cool completely in the pan, about 2 hours.

*Yield — 20 brownies*
*Fat per brownie — 0.30 g.*

# 9

# *Sauces,* DRESSINGS, *and Condiments*

# Sauces

## Roasted Banana Sauce

One 8-ounce banana, unpeeled  
½ teaspoon freshly squeezed lemon juice

2 teaspoons light rum

Preheat the oven to 350 degrees.

Roast the banana in the oven until it softens and turns black, about 15 minutes.

When cool enough to handle, peel the banana and mash the flesh with a fork. Beat in the lemon juice and rum.

Serve immediately.

Yield—½ cup  
Fat per tablespoon—0.09 g.

The pale hue of roasted bananas is dramatic atop our deep, dark Flourless Chocolate Cake (page 149).

# Rum-Raisin Sauce

Goes well with Orange-Buttermilk Ice Cream (page 166).

¼ cup seedless raisins
¾ cup water
1 tablespoon light corn syrup

¼ cup light rum
1 teaspoon cornstarch dissolved in
2 teaspoons water

Combine the raisins and the water in a small saucepan. Bring to a boil over medium heat. Lower the heat and simmer for about 20 minutes, uncovered, until the raisins are plump and soft.

Whisk in the corn syrup and bring back to a simmer, which should take about 1 minute. Whisk in the rum and the cornstarch mixture. Continue to cook, whisking constantly, for about 1 minute more, until the sauce is clear and thick. Do not allow it to come to a boil.

Serve warm.

*Yield — ⅔ cup*
*Fat per tablespoon — Less than 0.01 g.*

# Cinnamon Cream Topping

½ cup nonfat vanilla yogurt
¼ cup evaporated skim milk, chilled

½ teaspoon ground cinnamon
2 tablespoons confectioners sugar

Combine the yogurt, evaporated milk, and cinnamon in a mixing bowl. Beat for about 1 minute with an electric mixer at medium speed. Gradually beat in the sugar.

Serve at room temperature or chilled.

*Yield — 1 cup*
*Fat per tablespoon — 0.02 g.*

We like this silky sauce on Apple Upside-Down Cake or Individual Peach and Sour Cherry Strudel (page 156 or 154).

# Mixed Berry Sauce

Serve this on Flourless Chocolate Cake, Poached Pears, or Orange-Buttermilk Ice Cream (page 177, 163, or 166).

⅔ cup hulled, quartered strawberries (about 4 ounces)
⅔ cup raspberries (about 4 ounces)

½ teaspoon freshly squeezed lemon juice
1½ tablespoons confectioners sugar

Combine all the ingredients in a blender or food processor and puree.

*Yield — ¾ cup*
*Fat per tablespoon — 0.08 g.*

# Garlic Sauce

1 cup 99% Fat-Free Chicken Stock
   (page 10)
10 cloves garlic (about 2 ounces)

½ cup buttermilk
1 teaspoon cornstarch
2 teaspoons water

Combine the chicken stock and garlic in a saucepan and bring to a boil over medium heat. Lower the heat, cover, and simmer for about 25 minutes, until the garlic is soft.

Transfer to a food processor or blender and puree to a smooth consistency.

Return the puree to the saucepan over low heat. Whisk in the buttermilk and cook for 1 to 2 minutes, just until the mixture begins to bubble around the edges. Remove from the heat.

Whisk the cornstarch and water together in a small bowl and then whisk into the garlic sauce.

Return to the heat and cook for 2 to 3 minutes longer, until the sauce thickens. Serve hot.

*Yield — ¾ cup*
*Fat per tablespoon — 0.10 g.*

An intense sauce that complements smoked poultry.

# Celery Sauce

This works well with Fish Sausage (page 18), as an alternative to the fennel sauce.

1¾ pounds celery, trimmed
¼ cup peeled, shredded celery root
6 teaspoons water
1 tablespoon cornstarch

1 teaspoon freshly squeezed lemon juice
½ teaspoon ground cardamom
⅛ teaspoon white pepper

Put the celery through a juice extractor. (This should yield about 2 cups juice.)

Combine the celery juice and celery root in a small saucepan and bring to a boil over low heat.

Meanwhile, whisk the water and cornstarch together.

When the juice comes to a boil, whisk in the lemon juice and spices. Remove from the heat and whisk in the cornstarch mixture. Return to heat and bring back just to a boil. Serve immediately.

*Yield—2 cups*
*Fat per tablespoon—0.04 g.*

# Spicy Carrot Sauce

2 pounds carrots (about 6 large carrots), trimmed
2 teaspoons freshly squeezed orange juice
1 teaspoon freshly grated ginger

2 teaspoons cornstarch
4 teaspoons water
Pinch of cayenne pepper
1 tablespoon chopped fresh cilantro

Put the carrots through a juice extractor. (This should yield about 2 cups of carrot juice.)

Combine the carrot juice, orange juice, and ginger in a saucepan and bring just to a boil over low heat. This should take about 5 minutes.

Meanwhile, whisk the cornstarch and water together in a small bowl.

When the juice comes to a boil, remove it from the heat and whisk in the cornstarch mixture. Return to the heat and continue to whisk until bubbly. Whisk in the cayenne pepper and cilantro and cook for 1 minute more. Serve hot.

*Yield—2 cups*
*Fat per tablespoon—0.06 g.*

Works well with shellfish, especially shrimp and scallops.

This works
extremely well on
Grilled Potato Salad
(page 74).

# Dressings

## Mustard-Buttermilk Dressing

½ cup buttermilk
1 teaspoon light corn syrup
1 tablespoon white wine vinegar
½ tablespoon freshly squeezed lemon juice

1 clove garlic, halved
½ teaspoon mustard powder
¼ teaspoon salt
⅛ teaspoon freshly ground black pepper

Combine all the ingredients in a blender and puree to a smooth consistency.

*Yield — ½ cup*
*Fat per tablespoon — 0.19 g.*

# Honey-Mustard Dressing

2 teaspoons Dijon mustard
2 tablespoons honey

½ cup apple juice
1 teaspoon chopped fresh thyme

Combine all the ingredients and mix until well blended.

*Yield — ½ cup*
*Fat per tablespoon — 0.13 g.*

Try this on Tossed Jicama and Snap-Pea Salad (page 68).

# Zucchini Dressing

Serve on sliced tomatoes, a medley of thinly sliced squashes, or green salads.

2 medium zucchini (about 1 pound total),
    peeled and quartered lengthwise
½ cup buttermilk
2 teaspoons light corn syrup
1 teaspoon finely chopped garlic
    (1–1½ cloves)

1 teaspoon dried oregano
⅛ teaspoon freshly ground black pepper
¼ teaspoon salt

Put the zucchini through a juice extractor. (This should yield about 1 cup juice.)

Combine the zucchini juice with the remaining ingredients and mix until thoroughly blended.

*Yield — 1½ cups*
*Fat per tablespoon — 0.07 g.*

# Honey-Ginger Dressing

½ cup honey
1 teaspoon freshly grated ginger
2 tablespoons apple juice

1 tablespoon freshly squeezed lemon juice
2 teaspoons finely chopped fresh mint

Combine all the ingredients and whisk thoroughly.

*Yield — ¾ cup*
*Fat per tablespoon — Less than 0.01 g.*

Try this on Papaya and Watercress Salad (page 62).

# Southwestern Ranch Dressing

Use this spicy dressing with your favorite leafy green salad.

1 cup buttermilk
2 teaspoons light corn syrup
2 tablespoons freshly squeezed lemon juice
2 tablespoons chopped fresh cilantro

1 teaspoon chili powder
⅛ teaspoon white pepper
Dash of salt
4 drops of hot sauce

Combine all the ingredients and whisk thoroughly.

*Yield—1 cup*
*Fat per tablespoon—0.09 g.*

# Orange-Honey Dressing

½ cup freshly squeezed orange juice
2 tablespoons honey
1 tablespoon champagne vinegar

1 teaspoon light corn syrup
½ teaspoon coarse kosher salt
½ teaspoon freshly ground black pepper

Combine all the ingredients and whisk thoroughly.

*Yield — ¾ cup*
*Fat per tablespoon — 0.04 g.*

Pair this dressing with Orange-Watercress Salad (page 71).

This is based on the Victorian "catsups," which were savory spreads bearing little resemblance to today's commercial tomato catsup. The spicy pumpkin flavor blends exceptionally well with cold turkey or chicken. Bottled onion juice is available for those without juice extractors.

# Condiments

## Spicy Pumpkin Catsup

*One 6-ounce white onion, quartered*
*1 cup pure pumpkin puree*
*   (not pie filling)*
*½ cup water*
*¼ cup apple cider vinegar*
*2 tablespoons apple juice*
*1½ tablespoons honey*

*⅛ teaspoon freshly grated ginger*
*¼ teaspoon ground cloves*
*½ teaspoon curry powder*
*⅛ teaspoon ground allspice*
*¼ teaspoon salt*
*⅛ teaspoon cayenne pepper*

Put the onion through a juice extractor. (This should yield about ¼ cup onion juice.)

Put the pumpkin in a small saucepan. Whisk in the water, onion juice, vinegar, and apple juice. Add all the remaining ingredients, stir, and simmer for about 20 minutes, uncovered. The mixture will be done when the water doesn't separate from a small portion removed to a plate.

Use hot as a sauce or refrigerate for 1 to 2 hours to thicken and serve chilled as a catsup. The catsup will keep for about a week in the refrigerator.

*Yield — 1½ cups*
*Fat per tablespoon — 0.02 g.*

# Sweet and Sour Red Onions

½ cup balsamic vinegar
½ cup sugar
1 cup thinly sliced red onion
  (about 1 small onion)

⅓ cup seeded, thinly sliced green bell pepper
½ cup seeded, thinly sliced yellow bell
  pepper

Combine the vinegar and sugar in a saucepan and bring to a boil over medium heat. Lower the heat and simmer for 5 minutes. Remove from the heat and cool for 10 minutes.

Combine the onion and peppers in a bowl. Pour the vinegar and sugar mixture over them. Leave at room temperature for 20 minutes, stirring occasionally, then refrigerate for at least 1 hour. Drain most of the liquid before serving.

*Yield — 1½ cups*
*Fat per tablespoon — 0.02 g.*

A pungent, chunky, homemade condiment. Try it with Potato Cakes (page 30) in lieu of the red pepper cream.

# Tarragon-Peach Chutney

1½ cups unpeeled chopped peaches (about 2 medium peaches)
¾ cup peeled, chopped pear
¾ cup peeled, chopped Granny Smith apple
1 tablespoon freshly squeezed lemon juice
¼ teaspoon grated lemon rind
¾ teaspoon finely grated fresh ginger

¼ cup tarragon vinegar
¼ cup dark brown sugar, firmly packed
¼ cup golden raisins
1 tablespoon chopped fresh parsley
¼ teaspoon dried tarragon
⅛ teaspoon ground cloves
⅛ teaspoon ground nutmeg
⅛ teaspoon ground allspice

Combine all the ingredients in a large heavy saucepan and mix well. Bring to a boil over medium heat. Reduce the heat and simmer for 30 to 35 minutes, uncovered, stirring frequently, until the chutney is thick.

Remove from the heat and cool. Serve chilled or at room temperature.

*Yield — 1¼ cups*
*Fat per tablespoon — 0.08 g.*

# Glazed Pearl Onions

12 ounces pearl onions
6 tablespoons honey

½ cup red wine vinegar

Bring a saucepan of water to a boil, add the onions, and boil for 3 minutes. Rinse under cold running water.

Trim the root on each onion. Grasp the root end and gently squeeze toward the stem until the onion slips out of its skin.

When the onions are peeled, put the honey in a small saucepan and cook for about 1 minute over low heat, until it liquefies. Stir in the vinegar. Cook, stirring, until well mixed, about 1 minute more.

Remove from the heat and stir in the onions. Cool to room temperature, then chill in the refrigerator for 2 to 3 hours.

*Yield—6 servings*
*Fat per serving—0.09 g.*

A chilled condiment that is best the day after it's made.

# Tomatillos and Cherry Tomatoes in Basil Vinegar

½ cup halved red cherry tomatoes
 (about 4 ounces)
½ cup halved yellow cherry tomatoes
1 cup quartered tomatillos (about
 4 tomatillos)
⅓ cup basil vinegar (see Pantry)

⅓ cup water
½ tablespoon coarse kosher salt
6 leaves fresh basil
2 thin lemon slices
1 clove garlic

Combine the tomatoes and tomatillos in a mixing bowl.

Put the basil vinegar, water, and salt in a saucepan over high heat. Bring to a boil, then remove from the heat and set aside to cool.

Stack the basil leaves on top of each other, roll into a long cylinder, and slice thin. Add the sliced basil and the lemon to the tomato mixture, then press in the garlic.

Pour the cooled vinegar liquid over the tomato mixture and toss to coat. Marinate for 2 hours at room temperature before refrigerating. Serve chilled.

*Yield — 8 servings*
*Fat per serving — 0.16 g.*

# Index